BEYOND INVINCIBLE

BEYOND
INVINCIBLE

Live **LARGE**, Live **LONG**, and
Leave a **PROFOUND** Legacy

JENNIFER L. CARROLL

NEW YORK

LONDON • NASHVILLE • MELBOURNE • VANCOUVER

Beyond Invincible

Live Large, Live Long, and Leave A Profound Legacy

Published in New York, New York, by Morgan James Publishing. Morgan James is a trademark of Morgan James, LLC. www.MorganJamesPublishing.com

The Morgan James Speakers Group can bring authors to your live event. For more information or to book an event visit The Morgan James Speakers Group at www.TheMorganJamesSpeakersGroup.com.

ISBN 9781683509226 paperback
ISBN 9781683509233 eBook
Library of Congress Control Number: 2017919482

Cover and Interior Design by:
Chris Treccani
www.3dogcreative.net

In an effort to support local communities, raise awareness and funds, Morgan James Publishing donates a percentage of all book sales for the life of each book to Habitat for Humanity Peninsula and Greater Williamsburg.

Get involved today! Visit
www.MorganJamesBuilds.com

This book is for you, Phil.

I wish you could have read it.
I believe it would have made a difference.
Thank you for living every day the Phil Carroll way, and leaving your legacy with us forever.
Your Phil-osophies of life continue to guide our journey facing forward.
You are proof positive that if you live large, love passionately, laugh out loud, learn each day, and lend a hand to those in need, you will leave a legacy of love.

You are beyond invincible.
I love you and miss you every day.

CONTENTS

INTRODUCTION

Welcome aboard the Beyond Invincible bus. You're about to embark on an incredible journey.

This journey has two distinct parts. In Part One, I'm going to introduce you to Phillip Carroll, a rock-star entrepreneur. You'll find out how he made his first million at the age of twenty-five and how he rode the highs and lows of the entrepreneurial roller coaster with great success.

You'll hear about our epic love affair and how he convinced me to say, "I do." You'll learn about the extraordinary family known as the Christmas Carrolls, and how great tragedy can bring great wisdom and perspective on living and dying. Phil and his family learned these tough life lessons many times over with people far too young and graves dug far too soon.

You'll learn the secrets of surviving and thriving in a long-term relationship with an entrepreneur. No marriage is perfect, but ours was remarkable for twenty-two years. I'll take you along with us as we traveled the world with our friends and family, and you'll learn how the most important things in life are not what you do but who you do it with.

And I'll share with you some of the parenting philosophies that helped guide our children to their own early success as young adults: our son, Austin, as a professional hockey player, and our daughter, Jessica, as a YouTube influencer and red-carpet reporter.

If you are an entrepreneur, you will probably identify with my late husband, Phil Carroll, even recognize yourself in him. You most likely have—or want to have—that same invincible entrepreneurial spirit. Yet Phil was stopped by prostate cancer at the age of fifty-two. This horrible disease slowly took Phil's manliness, his strength, his voice, his breath, and ultimately his life. My hope is that this is where your path will be much different from his—much longer.

And that leads us to the second part of the journey. In the first part, you get to settle in and watch the movie of our lives before cancer. But the second part isn't about the movie of Phil's life; it's about the movie of *yours*.

In Part Two, I share the lessons Phil taught us living while dying, which we came to call our Phil-osophies of life. My hope in sharing them is that you will come to appreciate that you are the star of your own movie. You are the hero of your own book.

If you met your end tomorrow, and your significant other was about to speak to a room full of your peers, or decided to write a book about *your* philosophies of life, what would your special person say? What would your story be? What role would you play in the movie of your life?

You may be wondering, "What on earth could this grieving widow possibly share with me that could make a difference in my life or the lives of the people I love?"

Good question. Now I have a question for you: Do you want to be invincible?

Eventually, we're all going to die. If we've had a birth-day, we're going to have a death-day carved on our tombstone. But what about the dash in the middle? How do we live that dash to leave our legacy?

I'm talking about the kind of invincible that will allow you to push that death date as far into the future as possible. I'm talking about the kind of invincible that will allow you to watch your daughter walk down the aisle at her wedding, the kind of invincible that will allow you to watch your son live out his dream, and the kind of invincible that will give you a chance to grow old with the person you love.

Do you want to be that kind of invincible?

Ninety-six percent of men survive prostate cancer, but Phil didn't. Although he was only forty-seven when he was diagnosed, he had waited too long. The truth was that Phil was not proactive about his health. He didn't believe in going to the doctor.

That means we learned one of the most important Phil-osophies of life only after Phil was gone: *get checked*. I couldn't bear it if you picked this book up and then put it down before you got to this Philo-sophy. If you don't read any other chapter of Part Two, please, read "Phil-osophy #8: Get Checked."

Phil might not have been as invincible as he thought. But you can be *truly* invincible if you apply these Phil-osophies to your life and share them with the people you love. You can not only live large, but live *long*—and leave a profound legacy.

So, jump aboard and take a seat. I know you're going to enjoy the ride. I sure did.

The Carrolls

||||||||||||||||||||||||||||||

PART ONE
Living Large

||||||||||||||||||||||||||||||

CHAPTER 1
My Rock-Star Entrepreneur

||||||||||||||||||||||||||||||||

I f you ask a couple how they met, if they've been together for any length of time, you'll likely hear two different stories. This is certainly true of Phil and me.

If you asked me, Jennifer Leigh Whidden, how I met Phillip John Carroll, I'd tell you that we met in 1983 at a celebrity fundraiser for the Special Olympics, in Banff, Alberta, Canada. I was nineteen years old and one of the model hosts welcoming international guests to the spectacular Banff Springs Hotel nestled in the heart of the Rocky Mountains. I'd describe waiting at the entrance of the grand ballroom, amidst the heavy velvet drapes and glittering chandeliers, scanning the red carpet to lock eyes with my favorite celebrities.

One by one, the stars arrived—with no Hollywood sparkle at all! Even my idol Mary Hart from *Entertainment Tonight* showed up in a beige turtleneck with a ponytail and no makeup! Where was the WOW? It was one celebrity sighting debacle after another. Until in cruised this guy with a mane of blond hair and a moustache to match. Immediately the room was illuminated by his presence and his buttery-gold silk blazer. Who was this man? He screamed rock star! He turned out to be a hugely successful, twenty-four-year-old Calgary entrepreneur—and my friend's boyfriend. Darn!

Now, if you asked Phil how he met me, he'd look you straight in the eye with great pride and confidence and say, "I met Jennifer in the shower . . . with two other models!"

Although Phil stretched the truth relentlessly—especially with his favorite shower story—it wasn't as X-rated as he insinuates. I'll indulge you with the full details of the shower story soon enough, but first you need to meet Phil Carroll.

A Born Entrepreneur

If you asked Phil to describe himself, he would say, "I'm a loving husband, father, son, athlete, businessman, world traveler, and lover of life!" However, if you shook Phil out of a deep sleep and yelled aggressively, "Who is Phil Carroll?" he would shout back, bleary-eyed, "I'M AN ENTREPRENEUR! GO BIG OR GO HOME!"

Phil was born to be a wild, fearless, rock-star entrepreneur. There are some things about entrepreneurship that can't be taught; they are inherited. He was, as they say, a chip off the old block— both his parents were entrepreneurs. His father, Lorne, owned and managed a hotel in Banff, Alberta, while his mom, Dolores, started her career in the hospitality industry and eventually owned and managed a landmark gift shop on Banff Avenue.

Lorne proudly boasts about Phil's first and infamous business, which he started at the age of eight. Like other youngsters he had chores around the house, and one of them was cutting the lawn of their one-story home in Calgary, Alberta. The Carrolls didn't have the typical, backbreaking, push mower—no, they had the state-of-the art, lime-green Lawn-Boy electric-start mower, and all the neighbors took notice. Little entrepreneur Phil recognized an opportunity and began soliciting the nosey neighbors to sign up for his lawn maintenance business. Phil became University Heights' official Lawn Boy, and he soon, due to high demand, began hiring his buddies to join his labor force. While most young boys his age were building Apollo 11 spaceships out of Legos and imagining their own heroic moon landing, Phil was calculating the profit margin of his neighborhood business venture. Dad didn't pay him for his chores, but the neighbors did!

Lorne recalls the day he was approached by neighbor Fred Perry, who, while driving home from work, was puzzled as he caught a glimpse of a strange boy, at a stranger's home, pushing his John Deere electric mower. Fred pulled over to inquire why this boy was cutting the neighbor's grass with *his* lawn mower. Without hesitation the boy said that he was working for Phil Carroll, and Phil gave him this lawn mower. A few days earlier, Phil had asked to borrow Fred's lawn mower. Fred assumed the Carrolls' lawn mower was broken, and so he did what any neighborly neighbor would do—he lent his mower to Phil. The reality was that Phil's business was booming and he needed more mowers, so he started to borrow them from his helpful neighbors. Fred got a kick out of this long-haired blond kid's ballsy move, so he kept lending Phil his lawn mower but negotiated a cut. When Lorne heard about

Phil's lawn dealings, all he could do was chuckle to himself about his son's brilliant entrepreneurial strategy.

Dolores, too, has a young Phil entrepreneur story. In his mid-teens, Phil was in line with a buddy at the local movie theatre when they overheard two guys talking about this great job delivering flowers for the Christmas holidays. Phil jumped out of line and headed straight to the Flower Shop and got the job. Excited about his new income source for the holidays, he raced home to share his good fortune with his biggest fan, his mom. He explained that all the shop had required was a driver's license and a heated van. Dolores squinted her eyes a touch before asking him, "And how do you intend to get a heated van? We don't have one." Phil waved off her comment and said confidently, "No worries, Mom—I just unbolted the backseat of your Lincoln, and voilà, a heated van!" One of Dolores's parenting philosophies for her five children was "never clip their wings," which made this another one of her many proud Phil moments.

The Buck-Off

Phil Carroll spent his life celebrating life. To Phil, life was one big party! He loved hosting soirées with his family and friends—the more, the merrier!—with music blaring from huge speakers, bottomless cocktails, lots of laughter, and his infamous toasts. He would raise his glass to honor his peeps and, in his boisterous vibrato, state what had become known as his motto: "In life, it's not what you do, it's who you do it with that makes all the difference. So, here's to you and . . . who you do!" Laughter, applause, and the clinking of glasses would erupt, and the party would resume until the wee hours.

Phil walked his talk—or in this case, his toast. All his life he collected remarkable people to share his journey of success and significance, and to party with like rock stars. Although I was Phil's only wife, I was not his only life partner. Dave Steele was his business partner for thirty years, and their relationship was like a second marriage—but with different benefits. This truly remarkable bromance included weddings, childbirth, world travel, summers on the lake, and missionary work. It also endured business losses, family tragedy, illness, caregiving, a gut-wrenching eulogy, and a final good-bye.

Phil and Dave met at the University of Calgary at the ripe old age of twenty-two. It was their last year in business school. Dave was the president of the university's ski club and its two hundred members, which was the only reason Phil went to meet him. You see, Phil had a plan to put his partying talents to work and host the biggest party in the history of the University of Calgary, and he was calling it the "Buck-Off." He needed partiers, and the ski club had the most members of any club at the university. Phil decided he was going to do the Buck-Off with Dave Steele, because he was the ticket to selling tickets!

"Looking back, that party was when I learned what kind of guy Phil was," Dave told me. "You see, he couldn't just have any party. We had four bands, and male and female mud-wrestling. We brought in the El Toro bucking machine from Gilley's Bar in Houston, Texas—the first time it had ever been brought out of Texas. There were wet T-shirt contests, and the weight of all the eager onlookers hanging from the ceiling rafters actually brought down the house—or rather, barn. Fortunately, no one was hurt, but we only ended up breaking even after paying for damages. But what a party! Through that experience, I knew that Phil and I could work together and make stuff happen." Dave said this with a huge smile plastered on his face.

"We learned that we could not only work together, but play together, too," he went on. "We became best friends."

So the Dave and Phil bromance began with a barn-burning Buck-Off party that still holds the title of the best party in the history of the University of Calgary. Their next adventure was to turn the art of partying and holidaying into a multimillion-dollar business, all before they turned twenty-five.

Three Buoys Houseboats

In January 1982, the two boys and their friend, Rob Jensen, went on a weekend ski trip to British Columbia. En route, they stopped in the small town of Sicamous on the eastern shore of Shuswap Lake, which had the distinction of being the houseboat capital of Canada. A frozen fleet of a dozen houseboats piqued their curiosity. "Now, that would be an awesome party boat for next summer's getaway!" the three boys marveled. Phil noted that they would have to add a huge stereo and coolers, of course, to rock those boats. Completely pumped, the boys were astonished to hear that all the boats were booked for the next two summers.

Intrigued, they inquired at three other local houseboat companies, only to discover the same scenario: everything was booked. In college, the boys had learned one of the most important economic principles: when demand exceeds supply, there is a business opportunity.

Rob studied the boats carefully, and with his extensive twenty-two-year-old handyman skills, announced confidently, "Hey, I could make one of these boats easy," which ignited a blowtorch in Phil's entrepreneurial mind.

That was it! The aha moment when Phil decided he and his buddies were going to build a houseboat of their own. They jumped back into their van and were headed for the slopes, when something caught Phil's eye. He suddenly veered off the freeway down a dirt road and right into a farmer's yard. Without explanation, he jumped out of the car in front of an old, rickety Quonset hut filled with hay. He ran up to the door of the farmer's house and started pounding, until a less-than-impressed farmer answered, holding a shotgun. Dave and Rob quickly jumped up on the porch to make peace after Phil rattled the roost, and before they knew it, they found themselves in the midst of an amicable rental negotiation of fifty dollars a month for the farmer's Quonset hut. There it was, their perfect, affordable, houseboat building warehouse. They shook hands with the farmer and told him to clear out the hay, for they'd be back with building supplies in a couple of weeks.

Dave explained, "Our ski trip was not about to happen. Phil was on a mission. We turned around, drove back to Sicamous, went down the main strip of town, and found a one-acre waterfront property for sale for $100,000. We needed a $3,000 deposit, so we scraped our money together and wrote the realtor a check. We had just bought our first marina. On that one day, bound for the ski slopes, a sequence of events transformed our lives forever. In the course of forty-eight hours, without knowing anything about the houseboating business, we found ourselves driving back to Calgary with a farmer's Quonset hut for our factory, a marina to house the boats, and a general contractor to build them."

Dave and Phil continued working their nine-to-five finance jobs every week until five o'clock Friday, when they would shed their suits and ties, jump into their white Riviera, and bee-line it six hours to their Quonset hut warehouse in Shuswap. On the drive, they would strategize about raising the capital, designing and constructing the boats, and developing the business plan. All weekend they would work with Rob, building their houseboat, with Journey blaring, "Don't Stop Believin'," from the boom-box speakers. With the celebratory clinking of Molson Canadian, Three Buoys Houseboat Vacations was born.

Just like the Buck-Off had to be an epic party, Three Buoys Houseboats had to be an epic houseboat experience. In fact, they were about to launch the world's first floating luxury entertainment centers.

"Phil had to build a sexy boat and then offer a complete holiday experience. Even the first two boats had a railing on the top deck, complete with sun chairs, a huge beer cooler, and more importantly, a sound system that would rock the Shuswap waterways," remembered Dave. "The complete vacation package ended up somewhat like a mini Club Med experience. We had activities and games like parasailing, waterskiing, jetskiing, campfires, and skit nights. Many times groups of houseboats would tie up together and become a massive floating party."

For the next two summers, those two sexy houseboats were sold out. After just two years of houseboat rentals, they were in business.

"Sold out" meant that Three Buoys needed more inventory, which required three things: money, houseboats, and a brilliant business plan. Their first business strategy was to approach local Alberta banks for money to build hundreds of houseboats in the landlocked prairies. It was ludicrous. At bank after bank, the response was the same: a definitive NO, followed by a door slam.

Back to the drawing board the boys went, but this time they were one boy short. Rob was approached by one of the established houseboat companies to run their boat building division and decided to jump ship. Dave and Phil agreed to give Rob one of the two houseboats, but they would keep ownership of the Three

Buoys name, marina, and warehouse. The three boys split with an amicable agreement.

Phil and Dave then devised a brilliant investment package, where individual investors could buy the houseboats as tax shelters by taking advantage of the seldom-used Canadian federal tax incentive to encourage the marine industry.

About this time, Phil's big brother, Randi, who was running a lucrative employment newspaper in Seattle, came up with a bright idea. With his clever publishing mindset and whimsical way with words, he said, "Boys, seeing is believing. You want the dough; you've got to give them a show."

So Phil went to Mama Carroll and borrowed $5,000 to charter a jet. The plan was to fly seven investors out to the Shuswap to wow them with their new, sexy, Club Med-style houseboat that their entrepreneurial crystal ball was telling them would soon revolutionize the houseboat industry.

That first investors' houseboat tour went down like the *Titanic*. It sunk, and deep. While seven investors, Dave, Phil, and brother Randi sat in the lush private jet, with bottles of Dom Pérignon chilling in the ice buckets, the pilot announced that there was a storm brewing in the interior of BC, and they were grounded. Dave told me, "It was the lowest point of our journey so far. Trying to get those busy corporate CEOs back for another flight was an unlikely proposition. It was the only time I felt that maybe this wasn't going to be."

After shaking the hands of all the potential investors, thinking they'd probably never see them again, Phil and Dave went for Chinese food. Phil got a fortune cookie, and it read, "Market your idea."

"Believe it or not," Dave recalled, "we both looked at each other and said, 'You know what? We put way too much into this to give up. We have to find a way to make this work.'"

Over the next few weeks, Dave and Phil set out to find seven more investors. According to Dave, the morning of the rescheduled flight "was the most beautiful sunny day, as if God was shining down from above to illuminate our vision for the world to see—or at least the seven investors. At the end of the day, landing back in Calgary, seven investors handed us checks for half a million dollars, and we proudly popped the chilled Dom Pérignon with a toast."

Randi and his marketing genius officially came on board, and they were three boys once again. They worked in the basement of Phil's home, which became the Three Buoys Houseboat Vacations' official headquarters. It was time to hire their first employee. "We interviewed several girls," recounted Dave, "but this one gal, Brenda, stood out among the rest. In fact, she ended up asking us questions and interviewing us. She inquired about benefits." Dave laughed, remembering the look on her face when they bragged about having a fridge full of beer. Within ten minutes, Phil, the ever-so-spontaneous decision maker, said, "Man, this gal is just unbelievable. We've got to hire her."

But there was a hitch, as Dave tells the story: "She started the next day as a receptionist/secretary, and when we handed her the to-do list, she looked at us and said, 'Guys, I need to tell you something. I can't type.'" They had just hired their first secretary and found out five minutes after she started that she completely missed the job criteria. Brenda remained their number one employee and dear friend, and she eventually took over the entire operation of Three Buoys Houseboats with her husband, Gordon, whom she met through Three Buoys.

Rich as Cheesecake

Like all entrepreneurial ventures, the Three Buoys Houseboat journey had lots of ups and downs. One of the biggest ups was the media attention the company got because it had the three young, single, vivacious men at the helm. The media was all over these golden boys from Alberta, who were selling hundreds of boats to wealthy prairie investors. It was a broadcaster's rags-to-riches dream story. Only four years after leasing the farmer's Quonset to build their first boat, Dave and Phil appeared in the September 22, 1986, issue of *Forbes* magazine, which boasted, "To date, Three Buoys has sold some $29 million worth of houseboats."

During one of his first interviews on national television, Phil, then twenty-three, crowed with confidence, "All we want to do is see lakes across the world filled with houseboats—with the top decks covered with beautiful bodies in bathing suits drinking their favorite cocktails."

Phil's life ambition was always to live life out loud and enjoy every minute of it—and he would hold nothing back in getting there. When Phil was asked by a reporter, "What message do you have for young entrepreneurs?" he answered, "Extraordinary determination! When the going gets tough, the tough get going."

Dave and Phil appeared in Canada's *Flare* magazine as "two of Canada's yummiest bachelors." They called themselves "professional players," and did they ever play hard and work hard. In *Calgary Magazine*, one 1986 headline announced, "Life's a Holiday! Phil Carroll is only 25 years old, single, and as rich as cheesecake. If you think Phil is a happy guy, you're absolutely right."

The magazine story goes on to explain how the two young entrepreneurs built and sold houseboats during a recession, sold to prairie province investors looking for tax shelters, and then rented the boats out to vacationers and managed them. In the end they had over ten marina rental operations in Canada and the United States, and even built and operated a fleet of luxury yachts in the British Virgin Islands, with over four hundred employees. One of Three Buoys' claims to fame came after they finished building their twelve-hundredth boat and officially held the largest fleet of boats in the world—even more than the US Navy.

In the fall of 1987, as Three Buoys was set to file their IPO (Initial Public Offering) to go public on the Toronto Stock Exchange, Black Monday blindsided the world and derailed their plans of expansion. Shortly after the infamous stock market crash, the company was sold to one of the biggest RV vacation rental companies in North America, and Three Buoys Houseboat Vacations sailed off course.

Dave and Phil carried on their partnership, and over the course of thirty years would start and operate over a dozen businesses, including a fifteen-year stretch when they bought and sold over a billion dollars' worth of residential real estate.

In a closing scene of an hour-long CBC documentary on the Three Buoys story, Dave and Phil sat by a campfire, and Dave said as he pointed to the camera, "If you're going to do a business deal, make sure it's a big deal, because it's going to take you just as much effort and time to do a big deal as it will to do a small deal." Then Phil added boisterously, "We've always said . . . GO BIG OR GO HOME!"

CHAPTER 2

A Great Love Affair

||||||||||||||||||||||||||||||

As promised, I will now elaborate on the infamous shower scene and how it led to an unlikely love affair that lasted more than twenty-four years. On the night of the Special Olympics celebrity fundraiser when I first met Phil, he seized the opportunity to hire several models working the event, and I was one of them. He wanted us for the upcoming photo shoot he had scheduled the next weekend for Three Buoys' first brochure. Phil enthusiastically explained that all we'd have to do is prance around in bikinis for four days on their houseboats at the beautiful Shuswap Lake. Not a bad gig!

Again, I was only nineteen at the time, and I had spent my life to that point as a competitive figure skater. Did I mention I was

Canadian? Canadian children don't get bikes when they turn seven years old, they get skates—hockey or figure. I chose the latter, and I went to a self-directed learning high school for athletes so I could train half the day and right through the evening. Instead of partying with my friends on the weekends, like most teenagers my age, I spent most of my time at a luxury country club honing my talents, under the guidance of my coach Greg Folk, with aspirations of magically gliding my way to Olympic glory or Ice Capades stardom.

Dad was a well-respected plastic surgeon, and Mom was a sophisticated former model turned special needs educator. I was raised to be a proper young lady, educated and driven. I was the good girl, like Sandy from *Grease*, "lousy with virginity." My sister and I were known as the Forbidden Whiddens.

That's not to say we weren't social—I remember many nights spent with my crazy extended family and friends, drinking rum and cokes, playing gin rummy, and telling colorful stories around the massive oak table my grandpa built, until the wee hours of the morning. I loved waterskiing at our family cabin on the lake, taking my brother and sister tubing behind our boat, hiking in the wilderness with Dad, shopping with Mom, and giggling about boys with my figure-skating friends at slumber parties.

A chronic foot injury ended my skating career, and that's what led me into my fallback and short-lived modeling vocation. Although I did have boyfriends, I lived in a rather sheltered bubble compared to Phil Carroll—and in one long weekend photo shoot aboard houseboats, my bubble popped. My cherry remained unblemished, but my wild child alter ego was about to be unleashed by one of the Three Buoys.

Within moments after our luxury houseboat laden with models, photographers, promoters, and owners pulled away from the dock, the music was cranked up, the bellybutton shooters started, the clothes dropped off, and I witnessed my first skinny-dipping extravaganza. I stood—heart pounding, wide-eyed, guzzling my white wine spritzer—and watched as a boat full of strangers dropped their drawers, tossed their tops, and dove off the side of the houseboat into the chilly water below.

The only other person not participating in the late-night dip was a lone camera guy who was eagerly capturing the scene on his 35mm analog camera. Periodically glancing over at me, he'd flash me a wide-eyed drunken smile in the midst of his photo shoot. It was during those shenanigans that I got my first glimpse of naked men and all the eye candy that went with it. Oh, and I knew it was cold water, because I could see the proof with my own eyes.

Pickle Dish

The boats had two bedrooms in the main cabin and a penthouse loft on the top deck. The kitchen table even converted into a queen bed. Because I was a newbie to this partying-naked-skinny-dipping scene, I chose to sleep on the single couch with several layers of clothes and two blankets tucked in tightly all around me and pulled up under my chin.

The next scene was right out of the movie *Animal House*. I felt someone crawling in behind me and under my tightly tucked double layer of covers. I panicked and immediately gave him the best Hitman Hart elbow smash I could muster, right into his ribs. He rolled over on the floor, coughing and hacking, as I jumped up to see who it was. There lay the cameraman who had kept smiling at me all night in his pickle-dish-like Speedo swimsuit that left nothing up to the imagination whatsoever. I remember thinking he was rather cute and extremely well favored by nature, but had an odd fashion sense. Not only was he in the world's smallest swimsuit, but he wore white knee socks and sneakers to boot. It was definitely an image not easily erased.

I'm happy to say I had no other visitors over the next three nights. Speedo boy kept wearing his pickle-dish swimsuit the entire weekend, with those knee socks and white and red Nike sneakers, but he now had a bright purple bruise on his ribs to remind him that this girl didn't like pickles in her sandwich.

I caught on to this partying thing rather quickly, probably because Phil and Dave were such good teachers. I learned that the fundamentals of a good party were high-energy music played as loud as possible, scantily dressed participants, free-flowing cocktails, and lots and lots of laughing. I also think being in the hot sun in the middle of a lake on a floating house with no worries in the world didn't hurt.

The last night of the four-day partying escapade, Phil and Dave asked us models to get all dolled up because they were going to treat us and the photographers to a dinner in town.

As we were getting gussied up in the small houseboat bathroom, Phil walked in, dropped his drawers, and jumped in the shower with a big smile on his face. I looked around and said, "Come on, girls. You know he's going to be bragging about this forever. Let's give him something to boast about." That's right, I, Jennifer the virgin, who had not yet even skinny-dipped, came up with this audacious idea. We all dropped our dresses and jumped in the shower with Phil.

Like I said before, it wasn't as X-rated as you might think. Yes, it did involve three young, naked single women, and yes, there was a fair bit of lathering, but overall the scene was short-lived and somewhat innocent. And that, my friends, is the infamous shower story in all its glory.

Let me interrupt this chapter briefly to fast-forward five years: Phil and I are married and have a brand-new baby daughter. He wanted me to meet Dave Steele's brother, Peter, and his family. So we had them over for dinner. The doorbell rang, I answered, and the minute I saw Peter, I recognized him. I wasn't sure where or how, but I knew, somehow, I knew that face. Peter said, "No, no, no. We've never met before," and brushed it off as he introduced me to his darling wife, Barb, and his son, who was the same age as our daughter, Jessica.

The kids played together on the floor with our new puppy, Buddy, and we had cocktails and hors d'oeuvres.

I kept staring at Peter, racking my brain as to how I knew him. I never forgot a face, especially one as handsome as his. Then, as he reached for a mini gherkin from the antipasto platter, I had a huge epiphany. He was the pickle dish guy! He was the guy in the Speedo with the knee socks and sneakers I elbow-smashed on the houseboat photo shoot. I kept my aha to myself and chuckled under my breath as I played back the image of him in my head. I never knew that the fashion disaster in a Speedo hammock was, in fact, Peter Steele, Dave Steele's brother. I couldn't say anything at the time, but Phil and I both died laughing after Peter left when I told Phil my story. Through the years, that pickle dish story came out many times at parties—with Dave, Phil, and Peter, along with all of our friends, cracking up every time!

Playboy Phil's Miss June

Although I did experience Phil in the shower with two other models, there was no real spark between us yet—only soap lather. He fascinated me, but he was my employer for the weekend. Besides, I was a young girl who had dreams of TV journalism fame and fortune. So I took the invaluable partying skills I learned that legendary weekend on the houseboats and went off to follow my dream at Arizona State University and the Walter Cronkite School of Journalism and Telecommunication.

Phil went on to build hundreds of houseboats and become a Canadian entrepreneurial celebrity. He was typically spotted out with a girl under each arm and a bottle of Dom in each hand.

I graduated from journalism school, and one of the first jobs I got was during the 1988 Olympics in my hometown of Calgary. Because of my figure-skating background, I was able to get a job as the assistant to the figure-skating color commentators. For a month I worked alongside CTV's Michael Lansburg and reported to him the upcoming elements of each competitor's program. He was a talented broadcaster, and I admit I had a big crush on him, but he had no idea of the difference between a triple salchow and a double lutz combination—and I did.

I remember being in the rink-side media box, and in the midst of Brian Boitano's short program, I heard some distracting tapping on the glass behind me. It was Phil Carroll, with his mane of blond hair and matching mustache, in a perfectly tailored overcoat. "Hi, Jennifer."

Michael, who was in the middle of his live commentary, shot me a disapproving look. He was watching Brian setting up for another jump, and he needed my play-by-play. "I'm working, Phil," I whispered. "I really can't talk right now."

"Okay, give me your phone number." I quickly scribbled it down on a piece of paper and slipped it between the glass panels, as the audience behind Phil gestured for him to sit down and get out of the way.

He had such a playboy reputation that I didn't really expect him to call me, but I was wrong. A few weeks after my Olympic job ended, Phil took me on a date to Bow Falls in Banff, Alberta, where we sat outside, bundled in blankets, and had a picnic-basket lunch with the raging waterfalls as our backdrop. I couldn't help but reminisce about the shower scene. The date was magical. I found Phil so fascinating, and he lived such an exciting life. He also seemed genuinely interested in me and my career as well.

Phil and I dated for a few months after that, and I used to joke that I was Miss May, and then Miss June—with the slight possibility of becoming Miss July. I wasn't looking for a husband; I was a girl who just wanted some fun, and that was Phil's middle name! There was never a dull moment with Phil, and I loved his energy.

That summer, I took off with my younger sister, Tara, on a college graduation trip to Europe. My parents wanted us to explore the world before I began my broadcasting job and Tara went off to law school. Over the next six weeks, we traveled to thirteen different countries, and I sent Phil a postcard from every single one, sealed with a kiss. Now it was my turn to impress Phil, as I shared my exciting adventures cruising the Greek Isles, hiking the Swiss Alps, exploring the Roman ruins, climbing the Eiffel Tower, drinking a pint in London, and his favorite, topless tanning in Cannes.

I returned to start my new job in Winnipeg, Manitoba—nicknamed "Winterpeg," because it is the coldest place on the planet, or so it felt. I was the host of an entertainment show called the *Molson Entertainment Report*. Phil loved that I was ambitious and had dreams of making big things happen in my life, like he did in his. We dated long distance for well over a year. He'd fly in on the weekends, and we'd go to every musical, every rock concert, every ballet, and every comedy club that we could. For the first time in his life, someone else was showing Phil Carroll a good time, and he liked it.

One day, I showed up at the station to find a package addressed to me from Phil. Inside was an airline ticket to Rio de Janeiro for a week. My new boss at CKY-TV, Vivian Merkley, adored me. I was kind of the daughter she never had. We used to go for lunch and giggle about men, and she loved that I was dating this Canadian celebrity entrepreneur houseboat tycoon. When I showed her the Rio ticket, she gave me the week off, no hesitation—but when I got back, she wanted a full report, not for television, but for our lunchtime gossip.

I never realized all that time I was in Winnipeg, working on my own career, Phil was struggling to keep his Three Buoys empire afloat. He didn't share the details with me, and I didn't really ask. I remember learning about the Three Buoys bank takeover in my newsroom, watching it on television with everybody else. Phil went dark for several weeks. I couldn't reach him. Although I hadn't yet read John Grey's brilliant book *Men Are from Mars, Women Are from Venus,* I instinctively knew he was in his man cave, processing his stuff.

They say when one ship sinks, another sets sail, or something like that. Phil realized that after losing Three Buoys, he had another love of his life—and that was me. He showed up one wintry Tuesday afternoon in the middle of my broadcast, wearing his tailored overcoat, with an armful of bright red roses. After the broadcast, I went up to him and kissed him as he handed me the two dozen roses and then reached into his coat pocket and pulled out a crinkled piece of paper. It was my name and phone number—from the Olympics. He looked at me and said, "Isn't it amazing how something so small can make such a big difference in my life?"

He stayed with me for a whole month, living in my tiny little 800-square-foot apartment, as he contemplated his next move.

One day he came to me and said that he wanted to travel the world for two months, and he wanted to do it with me.

Did I mention that the most spontaneous thing I had done to date was agree to go on a houseboat one weekend with a bunch of strangers? I can't just quit my career and fly off with this jet-set entrepreneur! I was going to be a big deal too one day, but I loved him, and I would probably lose him if I let him go. What was I going to do?

Phil was a Tony Robbins enthusiast—along with Ed Foreman, Zig Ziglar, Les Hewitt, and John Assaraf, to name a few. He followed all those motivational guys, reading their books and going to their seminars. Phil had even paid for me to attend a Brian Tracy seminar in Winnipeg. As I sat contemplating what life would be like after I dropped a Phil bomb into my well-planned future, I remembered a foolproof method for making tough decisions I learned at that seminar. I decided to try it out. First, you imagine the worst-case scenario for both choices, using as much emotional connection and visual detail as possible, and then base your decision on your reactions. So, I imagined Phil and I married with two kids, and running into my coworker Rod Black, who had become the top sportscaster for TSN Sports and was rich and famous. How would that make me feel? Would I regret walking away from my broadcasting career to follow Phil around the world? I might never break back into the ring.

I pondered that scenario without much emotional upset, and then I imagined in great detail the image of myself as a famous CBC newscaster, walking offset, out the back door of the studio. Much like the scene in *The Way We Were* with Barbra Streisand catching a glimpse of estranged lover Robert Redford across the street—but in my case, it was Phil with his beautiful wife and their two children. Just the thought of this rattled me to the bone.

I had to go on the trip and be with this man I loved. There was my answer. As much as I wanted my career, I realized, through the tears, I wanted Phil even more.

The next morning, I quit my job, and a few weeks and several immunization shots later, I set off to discover the world with My Entrepreneur. What I didn't know was that he had told his mom, "The woman I take on this trip I'm going to marry," and that Miss May turned Miss June turned Miss July was soon to become Mrs. Carroll.

Around the World in Sixty Days

We started our travels in Europe, and then went on to Asia, where we explored Indonesia, Malaysia, and Thailand. From there we went to Australia and drove up the Gold Coast, where we jumped on a dive boat for five days and dove the Great Barrier Reef. It was the most incredible experience of my life. I was falling in love.

I hadn't felt well for several days, and I attributed it to a travel bug—my stomach getting used to new foods. I honestly didn't think much of it. When we were in Hong Kong on our way home, we went to see a doctor, and he asked if I thought I might be pregnant. "Not possible. I'm on the pill—right?" I asked, feeling even queasier from his line of questioning. He took some blood, I peed in a cup, and Phil and I headed back to the hotel.

The next day, as we were watching an old subtitled James Bond movie, the phone rang. Phil answered, "Hello? Oh, hi, Doc," and without hesitation, he said, "Great!" with enormous delight. I took in a huge breath and let out a sigh of relief. See? I knew I wasn't pregnant. Jennifer "Forbidden Whidden" doesn't get pregnant. She was far too responsible for that.

I went to the bathroom and started running myself a bath. Phil came up behind me as I was looking at myself in the mirror and smiled, then put his hand gently on my tummy, kissed my cheek, and said calmly, "We're going to have a baby."

I burst into hysterical tears, which did not stop for the next four months. I did not want to have a baby. I wasn't even married. This was ludicrous. I was on the pill. How does this happen? Phil had overachieving sperm. That's the only thing that made any sense.

What happened next was unexpected for a woman who was expecting. It was the last night of our two-month adventure. Phil asked me to get dressed up because he wanted to take me out for a celebratory dinner. I almost vomited thinking about eating a full dinner. I got dressed in head-to-toe white, right down to my stockings and shoes. I literally looked like a nun. Maybe it was an overcompensating attempt to make myself feel more virtuous.

We drove up this winding road to a beautiful green park overlooking the concrete jungle of Hong Kong, with me stopping every couple turns to throw up. When we finally got to the top of the hill, I ran off to upchuck yet again. Meanwhile, the driver went into the trunk and handed Phil some roses. As I'm wiping my mouth, Phil slowly walked up, bent down on one knee, looked up at me, and said two profound words: "Marry me."

My first thought was, "I wish I had a mint." But as I gazed deeply into the eyes of this beautiful man with his arms full of roses, I flashed back to the phone call from the doctor hours before, and how Phil picked up the phone, heard my diagnosis, and then, without a second of hesitation, answered, "Great!" It wasn't, "Oh, okay . . . Gosh . . ." or "Hmm . . . that's interesting." There was nothing but confident elation. And so I looked down at this man whom I loved, kneeling at my feet, waiting for my answer. I smiled and responded with the only two words on my mind: "Great!" and "Yes!"

On our trip around the world, I had come to discover that Phil Carroll was the marrying type. That he was going to be an incredible husband and an even more remarkable father. But at the moment of his proposal, all I knew was this: He thought that my pregnancy with his child was "great." He thought I was great, and we were going to make great things happen together. Plus, forever more, he could brag about meeting the mother of his children in the shower . . . with two other models.

CHAPTER 3

The Christmas Carrolls

||||||||||||||||||||||||||||||||

Church was a new thing for me when I married Phil. I did not grow up with church in my life. I was raised by remarkable parents with high moral values who practiced most of what the church preached. Yet we didn't have God in our lives—or rather, we didn't recognize that we did.

Aside from visiting Notre Dame and St. Peter's Basilica during my trip to Europe, the first time I can remember going to church was on June 23, 1990, when I walked arm-in-arm with both my parents down the aisle of St. Mary's Cathedral to marry my Catholic altar boy in front of two hundred witnesses—and I was four months pregnant! Yet despite my obvious sins, lightning did not strike me down. I figured that was proof positive God welcomed me into His kingdom. No one knew our little secret, for it was well hidden under my gown, but I knew God did, and He let our special day play out like a fairy tale.

Jessica Ashley Carroll was born on October 31, 1990, at the Grace Hospital in Calgary, Alberta. In fact, my father was the chief of surgery at that fine hospital, and I was treated like a queen. My mom, Joanne, whom Phil called "Jo" for short, was initially a touch skeptical about my new rock-star-entrepreneur, nicknaming husband, but the moment she saw him holding our precious baby girl, that sliver of doubt dissipated forever. Jessica melted her dad into a huge blob of love, nonstop cooing, and tummy zerberts. On that howling Halloween night, just five months after I became Mrs. Phillip Carroll, our family tree started to blossom.

At Jessica's christening, the priest who had married us just a few months before announced nonchalantly that he had discovered through the years that "although most pregnancies take nine months, the first can come anytime." And with that, the elephant was out of the room, and despite her parents' sins, Jessica was welcomed into the Church, a place where I would come to find great peace and solace.

Our First Christmas

As a new member of the Carroll clan, I learned quickly that Christmas was particularly special to the Carrolls. It was a lot more than just eggnog, presents, mistletoe, and watching the movie *Home Alone* bundled up in onesies. The Carrolls were Catholic, and Christmas day was the day they celebrated the birth of their savior Jesus Christ.

Christmas was a special time to the Carrolls because it brought the family together to celebrate life, reconnect, and remember all the family members no longer with them. Our first Christmas, at the Carroll family's Christmas Eve celebration, we visited Queens Park Cemetery, bringing fragrant pine wreaths and poinsettias to decorate not only the grave sites of Dolores's parents and sister, but also of Dolores and Lorne's two daughters Dolorn and Maureen. As I held our new baby girl, Jessica, in my arms, I was overwhelmed by the realization that they had had to lay to rest not one but two of their children. It was beyond comprehension.

Their baby Maureen was only six months old when she passed away from pneumonia. Several years later the couple was blessed with their first son, Randi, and then a few years later with another daughter, Dolorn. Phil was number four, and then came baby sister, Lisa. Dolores and Lorne recalled the night they arrived in Hawaii for a romantic getaway when there was a knock on the door. It was the hotel manager with a telegram. Their twenty-one-year-old daughter, Dolorn, had been involved in a head-on collision with a drunk driver, who was driving the wrong way on a freeway off-ramp. She was killed instantly when the car burst into flames. Phil was nineteen at the time and the only relative in Calgary, so he had to make all the arrangements while his traumatized parents took the longest six-hour flight of their lives back home to bury their sweet Dolorn.

For the Carrolls, Christmas was a time of hope, of rekindling memories, and of tremendous gratitude for their blessings. The following Christmas Eve, in 1991, I remember standing in church with my beloved Phil on one side of me, holding our now one-year-old daughter, and Dolores and Lorne on the other side, singing their hearts out as they gazed up at the large wooden cross suspended over the altar. I marveled at how this remarkable family had endured such tragedy yet kept on living with so much passion, enthusiasm, and gratitude. Then came the epiphany! The elixir of their hope and serenity was God. Every time they walked into church, and tonight in particular, I witnessed the calm and peace that blanketed them as they reconnected with their children through scripture, memories, song, and the love of family and friends. I saw all the sorrow and pain melt away and the remarkable gift of grace infuse them with peace. The "Christmas Carrolls" brought God into my life. Through their strength and surrender, I saw God's grace bless them and shine light on the darkness—a darkness that was about to become even darker.

A Christmas Surprise

The next morning, on Christmas Day, after the children opened up their stockings, Phil's big brother, Randi, announced that he had a special surprise Christmas gift for the whole family. He had even called his five cousins to drive in from Calgary to join us. Without revealing the surprise, Randi told us to bundle up warmly for a day in the snow-covered Rocky Mountains. We drove twenty minutes into Canmore, right up to a huge private helicopter awaiting our arrival. Randi had arranged a picnic in the heart of Rundle Mountain, and we were about to be shuttled up in this six-passenger helicopter.

It started off magically. Three different groups were shuttled up to the mountain where there were picnic blankets laid out for us, Christmas music playing from a huge boom box, and hot chocolate and apple cider to warm us from the inside out. It was a big party on the mountain with Phil, Jessica, and me; Phil's parents; his sister, Lisa; brother, Randi, his wife, Nora, and their two kids; and the five Timmons cousins. We were all singing, dancing, and sharing stories for hours with lots of hugging, laughter, and tears of joyous noel. Phil had given Randi's eight-year-old son, Christopher, a kite for Christmas, and we all laughed as we watched them try to get this kite to take flight. The air was so dry and cold we could see our breath as we talked and laughed, and it was dead still, without the hint of a breeze. This was not the day for kite flying, but that sure didn't stop Uncle Phil. He and Christopher took turns running across the mountain slope with that brightly colored eagle kite that refused to fly.

The Memorial Stone

Dolores came over to me, tears of joy welling up in her eyes, and just held me. She said she was so happy, and that she had marked this glorious day with a landmark. She pointed over to a large, protruding rock that strangely stood alone on the side of this huge mountain. It was slightly taller than it was wide and had a flat surface. When I got up close, I saw that she had used another sharp stone to etch the name "Carroll" in big, bold letters across the top, then a plus sign, and under that, the name "Timmons." It did indeed memorialize our glorious Christmas party on the mountain. But its full significance would only be realized later.

As the helicopter engine started up for the first shuttle back to the base, I approached Phil with a favor. While we had just spent the most remarkable Christmas Eve and Christmas morning with his family, my parents were waiting with much anticipation for their first and only granddaughter to arrive to celebrate Christmas. Instead of going back with the third shuttle, could he come with us now so we could head into Calgary to see my family? Without hesitation, he kissed me lovingly, helped Jessica and I aboard the helicopter, along with his mother and father, turned to hug his big brother and thank him for the greatest Christmas gift ever, and climbed on board with us. As we took off, I remember watching the remaining Carrolls and Timmons as they danced and laughed and carried on the celebration on that beautiful mountainside on Christmas morning. It's an image I will have embedded in my mind's eye forever.

As we drove back to Calgary, the second shuttle took Randi's wife and kids, Lisa, and cousins Leslie and Nicole back to the base. A few hours after we arrived at my parents' house, there was a call for Phil. With a pale, blank expression, he walked up to me and said he was going to Canmore—did I want to come? Could Jessica stay with my parents? With no further explanation, I grabbed my coat, hugged my parents and Jessica, and followed Phil to the truck. The call had been from Phil's dad. The last helicopter hadn't returned. He had been waiting at the helipad base for hours, and he was worried. He had good reason to be.

To make a horrifically long and tragic story short, Phil did everything to convince the helicopter company and several private airplane charters to do a flying search-and-rescue into the mountain range, but night had fallen, and it was too dangerous. In authentic Christmas spirit, over twenty friends arrived dressed for subzero survival. Loaded up with backpacks full of turkey sandwiches, with Phil leading the brigade, they set out on foot into the mountain range in search of the missing. It wasn't until the break of dawn that they reached the crash site where the bodies of four passengers and a pilot lay motionless in the frozen tundra of Rundle Mountain.

Christmas morning 1991 started off so magically, celebrating life and love on the snow-covered Rocky Mountains, and quickly turned tragic with the loss of Phil's brother, Randi, and their three cousins, Allison, Deanne, and Greg. It's the ebb and flow of life, the yin and yang. A week later, Dolores and Lorne watched as a grave was dug for their third child, buried far too young, far too soon. I couldn't help but think back to Dolores's landmark and realize its uncanny similarity to a tombstone.

The Carrolls' resilience and faith are extraordinary. How can anyone truly empathize with the unimaginable horror they endured losing three of their children? Even then, I watched as their faith gave them the strength to carry on, and the tremendous love they had for their two remaining children and grandchildren is what continued to keep them out of the darkness. Dolores once told me that when she lost her first baby, she felt that the rest of her children would always be protected and safe. But after losing Dolorn and now Randi, she just prays for the best and enjoys every moment to the fullest, because no one is protected and life is not promised.

Family First

After the Christmas morning tragedy, Phil's primary focus shifted dramatically from business to family. Phil kicked into high-gear repair mode. So many lives shattered, so many broken pieces to pick up and rebuild. He became the rock of the family—not only for his parents and surviving sister, but also for Randi's widow, Nora, and his surviving cousins, Leslie and Nicole.

It was in the trenches of this brutally challenging time that Phil and I established our new life motto—Phil's standard toast—that it's not what you do but who you do it with that makes all the difference. Love is all that matters.

Phil and Dave were working diligently on clicking up the track of their new business venture, investment real estate, but family, friends, and faith rose to the top of their hierarchical pyramid of priorities. On Mother's Day that year, Phil handed me the key to a cabin on Skaha Lake in the beautiful Okanagan Valley of British Columbia, where we spent the next twenty-some summers together with our kids, relatives, and friends. Although

Phil worked hard at his businesses, he always left abundant time to play hard with his people.

With Phil, it was both quality *and* quantity of time—many long, hot days teaching his kids to ski and wakeboard on the boat with all their friends, biking around the vineyards and lakes, picking fruit from the surrounding orchards, and biting into the juiciest and sweetest fruits of life.

In 1992, Phil extended the family by joining an entrepreneurial networking group called Young Entrepreneur Organization (YEO). It later became known as Entrepreneur Organization (EO), due in part to the fact that the old founders wouldn't leave, so they dropped the "young." Over the years, we traveled to more than twenty-five different countries through the various Entrepreneur Organization's conferences and met most of our best friends through EO's global family of entrepreneurs. EO founder, Verne Harnish, and his darling wife, Julie, became lifelong friends to both of us, and the organization continues to welcome me with opportunities around the world to share the Phil-osophies of life with fellow entrepreneurs.

On March 26, 1994, our little family became a quartet when our son was born. I'll never forget what Phil said when our "human Mack truck" of a son arrived with his bowling-ball-sized head. "Is it a boy?" I demanded, barely conscious after my excruciating delivery. "It's . . . it's . . . it's . . . " he paused, as his voice quivered, "it's a hockey player!" As much as he loved his beautiful daughter, Jessica, that moment was unequivocally the happiest of his entire life.

With all the accomplishments Phil achieved, above all else he was a remarkable, hands-on Dad who rarely missed a game, dance recital, or school play—and never, ever let anything keep him from spending those magical twenty summers at the cabin, living life to the fullest with his family. I can't begin to express how profoundly those twenty summers of cherished memories continue to reverberate into our lives.

"Our Lives Are about to Change"

Phil and I traveled the world together, ran on the beaches, and loved dancing together. On our date nights, I'd get all dolled up for him—he called me a woman of a thousand looks.

Phil got a few hall passes from me each year. One was a heli-ski trip with his university buddies who called themselves "Team Deep," and the other was a boys' fishing trip with some investment banker buddies who would wager bets on the biggest catch.

One year on this fishing trip, after a few too many beers, he and his fellow fishermen were having a pissing contest off the side of the boat. (I've often heard men use the term "pissing contest," but I never realized that they do sometimes literally have pissing matches!) Phil, being the youngest one, was a little rattled by the fact that although he might've caught the biggest fish of the day, he definitely didn't win the pissing contest.

He also realized that he was urinating a lot more often than these older men, when his buddies kept teasing him about going down to the bathroom so often. However, Phil chose to ignore these symptoms. He thought, "I'm only forty-seven and as healthy as a whip. I eat organic, work out almost everyday, never smoked, drink only socially—and besides, I don't believe in going to the doctor."

In fact, he actually bragged about never going to the doctor or dentist. Phil knew his own body better than any doctor could. If he ever felt sick, he would just throw back a handful of vitamins, eat an apple, go for a jog, and voilà—he was all better.

Phil was invincible . . . until he wasn't. It took pressure from both Dave and me to finally get him to go get checked.

I was in a dentist chair getting my teeth cleaned when I got a call from Phil on my mobile. Unaware that he had gone to his doctor, I had decided to call him back after the cleaning. When Phil rang again, I knew something was up. The dentist rinsed out my mouth and took off my bib, and I walked outside to return Phil's call. "Jennifer, I need you to meet me at the doctor's office," he said, as my heart sank. "Our lives are about to change . . . I have prostate cancer."

IIIIIIIIIIIIIIIIIIIIIIIIIIIIIIIII

PART TWO

Lessons Learned Living While Dying

IIIIIIIIIIIIIIIIIIIIIIIIIIIIIIIII

Phil was right, of course. Our lives did change—completely and irrevocably. For the next five years, we were submersed in fighting for Phil's life. No part of us, of our family, or of our world remained untouched.

That's why when the journey was over, we were in awe to discover that Phil had applied the very same Phil-osophies of life to his dying as he did to living large.

Phil had become truer to these beliefs than ever, and with them, he became *beyond* invincible.

Part One might have been about Phil and our family, but Part Two is about you. As you read each chapter, I invite you to ask yourself: How can I apply this Phil-osophy to become truly invincible—for my business, my life, my family, my legacy?

PHIL-OSOPHY #1

Be Positive

||||||||||||||||||||||||||||||||||||

It's easy to be positive when life is going great, right? And if you're an entrepreneur, being positive is part of your DNA. But no one is insulated from challenge, chaos, or even catastrophe. How do we stay positive in the dark times?

How do we stay positive when we hear these words:

"I'm leaving."

"You're bankrupt."

"Your child has autism."

"You have stage four prostate cancer."

We do what Phil did: we grab our rose-colored glasses! Entrepreneurs always have a pair. When you look through them, you see endless opportunities, adventures, and possibilities. When you look at doors that were once closed, miraculously, a crack appears. I admired a lot of things about my late husband, but what impressed me most was his uncanny ability to see the positive in everything, everyone, and every situation. Whenever the kids would come to Phil and ask, "Dad, will you help me? I have a problem," he'd look at them and say, "The Carrolls don't have problems. We have opportunities. So, what's your opportunity?"

Try it. If you're facing a problem that feels insurmountable, ask yourself, "What's my opportunity?"

He was never, ever without his rose-colored glasses, even to his last breath.

One day, I had to take Phil to the hospital for his first of many blood transfusions. I was just sitting there, staring at this man I loved more than anyone in the world. He was lying on a hospital bed that was barely the size of him. His skin was gray, his body wasted. He had a tube up his nose, attached to an oxygen tank, and an IV in his arm hooked to all these monitors. Beeping equipment surrounded us. I just stared at him. I couldn't breathe.

Maybe you or your loved one has been in this position. If so, you know the feeling. It's numbing. It's surreal. It's a nightmare. *How can this be happening?* I thought.

Then suddenly, a husky nurse standing behind Phil yelled out with authority, "Be positive!" It rattled me. Wouldn't it have rattled you? Well, I looked at Phil. He looked at me. I looked up at her. I said, a little timidly, "Well, we *try* to be positive."

She tipped her head to the side, squinted at me, and said, "No, no, no, sweetie. I'm not talking to you. I'm talking to the nurse behind you. Yeah, I have to tell her your husband's blood type. He's B positive."

Of course he's B positive! All my life, I knew he was the most positive man alive—and there was the proof in his blood. Phil was elated to find out his blood type. He milked "B positive" for all it was worth, let me tell you. Phil stayed positive, too, to the very last day of his life, and I want to share some of the ways he did that.

Repel the Negative

To truly be positive, you have to first refuse to be negative—which is exactly what Phil did. He always thought of himself as a superhero with those bullet-deflecting wrist guards. As negative stuff came at him, he just stuck up his wrist guards and blocked those bullets. It was actually amazing to watch. If a movie we were watching became violent, it got shut off. If a friend or a visitor started to gossip—bing, bing! They were asked to zip up or head out.

If one of his doctors ever said something like, "This cancer is likely going to . . ." Phil would just get those bulletproof wrist guards up in his face and say, "Doc, I don't want to dwell on the negative. I only want to hear the positive." To some, it was denial. To Phil, it was grabbing his rose-colored glasses and living. He never dwelt on the negative and the "what ifs." He just focused on the "what's next."

Visualize Your Dreams

Not only did Phil actively repel anything negative, he also constantly filled his mind, body, and soul with positive visions of what he wanted in life.

When our kids were young, we always had them create vision boards—a corkboard with pictures of their dreams and aspirations. We'd place them on the wall in front of the toilet, where they probably did their best thinking, so that they would visualize the images of the things they dreamed of.

After one of my speaking engagements for the Entrepreneur Organization in Alberta, Canada, Jessica was approached by a couple of young entrepreneurs who asked her how we raised her and her brother to be such successful young adults. Here's what she said.

Our parents were always great role models for being positive and staying focused on our dreams and the life that we imagined for ourselves. They were all about visualization. They had us write out our goals every year, starting at the age of probably six. Then every year we would look back and review our goals. It's amazing how many we accomplished. And it wasn't just about setting goals. It was about the action steps to getting there.

Right before I went off to college, Mom and Dad had me take a workshop with them called Lifepilot that was created and hosted by one of Dad's mentors Peter Thomas. I did a vision board full of pictures of all the things I wanted to accomplish during college. Four years later, after I graduated from Chapman University with a Bachelor of Arts in Broadcast Journalism, sadly without my dad, I found it under my bed, and was overwhelmed to discover that I had accomplished every single thing on that vision board. It was incredible. There was a picture of a surfboard because I wanted to learn to surf, and I did learn how to wakesurf behind my boat at our cabin. I had a picture of a little white sports car, and I ended up buying almost exactly the same one.

The coolest example was that I put a picture of a girl on the E! News red carpet, and I actually ended up getting an internship at E! News.

My favorite image was one of my dad and me and beside it I had a picture of a globe. You see, I wanted to go on a daddy-daughter trip somewhere together. Dad and I hiked the Great Wall of China together, and I'll never forget it.

One of my dad's all-time famous quotes was, "Never lose sight of your childhood dreams." He lived that every single day, and my mom did, too. Visualizing, being positive, and staying focused on my dreams and the life I imagine is really the biggest lesson my parents taught Austin and me. My brother had a life-size picture of his favorite Calgary Flames player, Jerome Iginla, on his bedroom wall when he was six years old, and there was never a doubt in his mind that somehow, someday, he was going to get there, no matter what it took. He signed with the Calgary Flames in 2015.

Of course, Phil, during these challenging times with cancer, had his own massive vision board that took up the entire wall of his bathroom. It was covered with pictures of him celebrating life: snowboarding with his kids, dancing with his wife, traveling the world with his EO friends, running on the beaches in California with his puppies, watching his son's semi-pro hockey games, watching his daughter interviewing celebrities on the red carpet, scuba diving with her in Turks and Caicos, walking the beaches with his parents, surfing and partying on the boat with his friends and family, and playing hockey.

The vision board also contained positive words of affirmation, like, "Yes, you can do it!" "Just when the caterpillar thought the world was over, it became a butterfly," and "Love is appreciation for all that we do for each other." Phil would stare at this board as if it were his reality, dreaming of the day he would be healthy and strong once again.

Here's what Austin remembers:

Dad was a huge believer in visualization and the law of attraction. He was always encouraging us to send positive energy and thoughts into the world. We had dream boards and made positive affirmations. In the mornings, Dad would have us yell out, "Today's going to be a great day!" Visualization is one of the biggest gifts he left us.

The drive to my hockey games was all about visualization. Dad would turn the music we had playing off and then have me close my eyes as he described in detail the moves and plays I would make flawlessly on the ice. He always included at least one goal. When we started this routine, I was very young, and on most of the drives, I would end up daydreaming about the ice cream shakes he would buy my team after the big win. But on those rare times I really put my mind to work and visualized the plays and goals, I became a witness to just how powerful this tool can be. Now twenty-three years old and playing professional hockey, I put this gift my dad gave me to work every day, visualizing all

the great moves, plays, and goals I want to make in the
game to come. The times my dad and I spent visualizing
together made a bond we will never lose. It's something
I will always share with him.

One day, when Phil was extremely sick, our friends stayed with him and sent me on a snowboarding getaway for a day. I remember him telling me to record myself from the top of the mountain right down to the bottom, as if he was there with me. I recorded that video, and I was amazed at the joy it brought him over the next several months. He watched it over and over, feeling each turn on the mountain with me.

Do you feel bogged down by the challenges in your life? Are you losing sight of your dreams and what you love to do? If so, maybe you need a vision board. What images would you put on your vision board? What wise words do you need to see and remind yourself of on a daily basis?

Sadly, Phil never did snowboard again. But I know in my heart, because of that video, he did in fact snowboard dozens of times in his imagination. It was his way of living while dying: being positive and using the power of his mind. It was extraordinary. Phil was proof positive that even in the darkest of times, if you grab those rose-colored glasses, you can live large—even while dying.

One Fun Thing

As a caregiver to Phil (aka his "can-cierge"), I realized that in order to take care of him, I had to take care of myself. I'd religiously work out a couple of times a week, no matter how exhausted

I was. Sometimes I'd show up and pay my cute, buff, tattooed trainer, Jason VanHuelen, to sit with me as I sipped a cup of tea and bawled my eyes out. I remember one morning, as I was lifting weights over my head, Jason said to me very nonchalantly, "What fun thing are you doing today?" I looked at him dumbfounded. In my mind, I envisioned the day ahead: I would leave the gym, go home, put Phil and his wheelchair and his oxygen tank into the car, and drive him to the clinic for chemo, probably pulling over several times for him to throw up from nausea. I'd get him to chemo, deal with him and the nurses as they inevitably had difficulty with the IV needle, and finally endure six hours of waiting while that life-saving poison dripped into his body. I looked at my trainer and said, "I'm going to have to get back to you on that one."

As I kept working out, I suddenly remembered that it was Monday. It was *Bachelor* day! Every Monday night, Phil and I would watch *The Bachelor*—that crazy reality show about the guy who had twenty-five women gaga over him. He would relentlessly eliminate them one by one and eventually break all their hearts, except for one lucky girl. Then he would get down on one knee and propose, gallantly sacrificing his bachelorhood. You know, a good, uplifting show about real life. Most men would probably hate to admit that they watched *The Bachelor*, but the truth was I had no trouble convincing Phil because it involved twenty-five gorgeous women running around giggling in bikinis. Plus he got brownie points with the wife—and he knew a happy wife is a happy life. I looked at my trainer and said, "My one fun thing is that it's *Bachelor* night tonight, and I'm going to watch it with Phil."

Our typically horrific chemo day played out completely differently, merely because I focused on and visualized my One Fun Thing and looked forward to it all day. As we drove to the clinic, when Phil was feeling nauseated and wanted me to pull over, I quickly said, "Hey Phil, who do you think is going to get bumped off *The Bachelor* tonight?" His state seemed to change. We started to talk about this girl or that girl going home with a broken heart. Later, when he was complaining about getting stuck with the needle and that the nurse wasn't doing it quite right, I once again brought up the show and his favorite girl, who had a very large bustline and loved to play football. We started talking about her bouncing boobs and catching a pass from the Bachelor. Once again, his mental state changed.

Focusing on One Fun Thing transformed chemo day—the worst day of my week (and Phil's too, of course)—into something actually tolerable. Every morning after that, Phil and I would establish our One Fun Thing for that day. Sometimes it was watching our son's pro hockey game on the internet, or a Skype call with our daughter in college, or maybe a visit from a friend. It might be a walk around the yard with the puppies, or a swim in the pool. That daily habit of visualizing our One Fun Thing helped us get through some horrific, painfully dark days.

> How might choosing One Fun Thing to focus on every day help transform even your darkest, dreariest days into something bright and positive? Imagine the power of looking forward to it later in the day, and then reflecting back on it afterwards. What One Fun Thing can you do today?

The Sign

As Phil's cancierge, I definitely had to dig deep to find my rose-colored glasses more than once. One of those times was

Thanksgiving—and not just any Thanksgiving. It would be Phil's last. I wanted it to be special. Extraordinary! Family and friends had flown in, and of course Phil wanted to have our usual big Thanksgiving turkey dinner.

I was not up for cooking, so I called our local gourmet grocery store and ordered a Thanksgiving turkey dinner with all the trimmings, to be picked up at five o'clock sharp Thanksgiving day. Guests had arrived, the table was set, I was in my festive Thanksgiving attire, and off I went to pick up our delectable turkey feast.

I was waiting in line at AJ's deli department, with a whole bunch of other hungry customers, until a young guy wearing a white deli apron handed me a tinfoil roasting pan filled with my turkey dinner. As I took the pan from him, I realized it was *cold.*

I looked at the guy and said, "I ordered a cooked turkey–ready to go." He replied, "Sorry, ma'am, this is the only way we serve our turkeys." He added, "All you have to do is cook it for three to four hours."

All I could think about was the house full of people and Phil, all sitting around the table with forks and knives in their hands, waiting for a hot, steaming turkey with all the trimmings.

I have to admit, I was a lot stronger during Phil's cancer journey than I thought I could be. I had kept myself together pretty well—until then! Holding this uncooked turkey with all the trimmings, I had an absolute breakdown right there in the deli department of AJ's. "My husband has cancer—*sob*—this is his last Thanksgiving—*sob*—and he's hungry—*sob*—and waiting—*sob, sob!*"

The store manager scurried over with a box of Kleenex, sat me down, and got me some cold water. A cute little gal from the bakery started rubbing my back (everyone was on serious cleanup duty in the deli department). It was one of those moments when

I desperately needed my rose-colored glasses. With all the horrible challenges we had faced in the past year, this was a small bump in the road. A first-world problem!

How could I stay positive? I had to look for the signs that everything was going to be okay. With my shoulders back, and half of AJ's staff helping me and my cold turkey with all its trimmings to the car, I looked up in the sky and saw . . . a sign!

It said "CHIPOTLE!" And under it, in neon, red lights, "OPEN!"

That was it! My rose-colored glasses worked! We shoved the cold turkey with all its trimmings into my trunk. I walked across the parking lot to Chipotle and bought twelve of the biggest stuffed burritos they could make, with all the trimmings, drove home with bags of steaming hot dinner, and we all enjoyed an extremely thankful Thanksgiving.

It was extraordinary!

No matter what challenges you face in your life, and no matter how dark times may get, remember to be positive. Grab those rose-colored glasses and your bulletproof wrist guards, repel the negative, visualize the positive, and find One Fun Thing to focus on each day. Be invincible. No matter what your blood type happens to be.

PHIL-OSOPHY #2

Stay Focused

||||||||||||||||||||||||||||||||

I t was summer 2012, and we were at home, deeply entrenched in Phil's cancer battle, when the doorbell rang and we received a package. Inside was a box of books, fresh off the printing press, titled *The Power of Focus: How to Hit Your Business, Personal, and Financial Targets with Confidence and Certainty,* written by Les Hewitt, Jack Canfield, and Mark Victor Hansen. As a longtime friend and business associate of Les Hewitt, Phil had been featured in one of the chapters, "Ideas to Make You Rich: Best Success Strategies."

Holding that book, at that time in Phil's life, was exactly what the doctor ordered. Face to face with his mortality, he held in his hand a piece of his legacy, and as he read through his chapter, I sensed his tremendous pride and confidence. Even though he was hooked to an oxygen tank, a wisp of the man he had been, I saw the radiance of the Phil I fell in love with two decades earlier.

I, too, read through the chapter. Although I've always been in awe of Phil's tremendous business accomplishments, I was more overwhelmed by the fact that the strategies he talked about in this chapter, which were key to his business success, were the same principles he now used in his cancer battle.

According to the book, here are his top three success strategies, which all have to do with the power of focus:

Pick Your Field and Stick with It

I learned this the hard way. As an entrepreneur, I had lots of ideas and I'd jump into things that looked exciting, that would ultimately distract me from my main focus. My strength is real estate, particularly buying and selling large condominium properties. It's important that you understand the industry that you're in. Learn everything about it, the players and the environment. Now my focus is on foreclosed homes. Properties. I still use the same strategies. You must see the biggest opportunities ahead of time and commit 100% when they arrive.

Phil Carroll, *The Power of Focus*

Phil started with floating real estate in Three Buoys Houseboat Vacations, then turned to landlocked real estate, and even at the end of his life when the housing market debacle hit hard, he found his niche in foreclosed properties. He was literally doing deals almost to the day he died.

As I looked over at Phil reading this book, I realized that he was now in the business of buying time. Before, his currency was money; now it was faith, love, and his "keep Phil alive" tribe. But the strategy of focus was the same.

Every morning he woke up with one thing in mind: 100 percent focus on health and healing. He worked out with a trainer several times a week. He'd do these hand-eye coordination drills to keep his mind sharp and get a little rhythm and balance back into his body.

He watched *The Secret* on DVD, which is about the power of visualization and how thoughts can change the direction of your life. His favorite part featured a cancer patient and showed an image of microscopic cancer cells literally dying off, one by one. Phil would watch this little segment every single day and afterwards sit and visualize his own cancer cells dying off, one by one.

He would go for daily walks, wheeling his oxygen tank behind him every step—every breath. He always said his body was meant to move, and as long as he was putting one foot in front of the other, he knew he was still alive and fighting.

> What field do you need to stick to? What is your unique ability? What gift do you need to share with the world, and are you spending time honing and mastering it? Are you focused on being the best you can be, in business and in health?

Les came to visit Phil toward the end of his battle. Peacefully sitting in the backyard together, Les talked about the impact Phil had on so many people.

"Your healing is taking place the way you focused on your business. It's really the power of focus that's going to make all the difference," Les said to Phil with encouragement.

Stick to Your Values

The number one priority for me is balance. When I am out of balance, life is more stressful and I lose focus. When my relationship with my wife and children is great and I'm healthy, my business flows better. I make sure I have regular breaks with my family. This is rejuvenating. When I go back to work, I can really turn on the adrenaline.

Phil Carroll, *The Power of Focus*

Phil always lived large, but he loved large and played large too, always leaving valuable time for the most important things in his life: his family, his faith, his friends, and his fitness. He was an entrepreneur through and through, and was very driven toward financial success, but his work success never got in the way of the things he valued most.

Phil was one of those entrepreneurs who literally never said no to anything. Even though he was older than me, he exhausted me with his full-throttle pace of living. He just couldn't pass up an opportunity to expand his business success *or* to experience life to the fullest. He was a life junkie. When Phil got invitations to four Christmas parties on the same night, he said yes to all of them—

and we went. Even with two kids, we were literally on an airplane every six weeks of our entire lives, going somewhere on a getaway. I learned to never put away the luggage, because as soon as I did, I'd just have to get it out again. It's as if he knew he had to cram a hundred years of life into fifty-two. I used to joke that I was glad he had a really great butt, because I spent my life following it.

About five years into our marriage, I attended a spiritual retreat with my girlfriends, where I discovered meditation and yoga for the first time. I was feeling so grounded and at peace. At this retreat, I had an epiphany that I wanted to simplify our lives somewhat. I wanted to say no to a few things. I learned the concepts of *KISS*—Keep It Somewhat Simple—and *staycation,* where instead of racing off around the world for your next adventure, you simply enjoy the tranquility of the beautiful home you created and each other. What a concept!

I wanted to share these ideas with Phil, so I booked a lunch date to talk to him—because back then that was the only way I could get his undivided attention—other than having sex. He showed up late and wound up, as usual, electrifying the room as he entered it. He was rubbing his hands together frantically, which is what he always did when he was pumped up and wanted to share something really exciting. Sometimes I even thought they'd start smoking.

He gave me a kiss, sat down, and blurted out, "I know you want to talk, sweetie, and I want to hear what you have to say, but first, I have to tell you what happened. It was like divine intervention. I've been feeling lately that my life's getting a little stagnant. I just need some kind of new adventure to liven me up a bit. You know?"

He stared at me, anticipating an equally enthusiastic response. He was met instead with a deer in the headlights gaze—yet he went on.

"You know our friends, Greg and Laurie Stemm from Florida? The treasure hunters? They dive down and bring up buried treasure?" I continued to stare dumbfounded, barely breathing. "Well, you won't believe this, but they just contacted me, and they're part of this excavation of a shipwreck thought to hold Spanish treasure off the coast of New Zealand, and in two weeks they're going, and they want us to come and be part of it. Isn't that exciting?"

I slowly put down my napkin, excused myself, and went to the bathroom, where I had the first official nervous breakdown of our marriage. As I looked at myself in the mirror, wiping the tears and mascara streaks off my face, I realized, "I'm married to an entrepreneur." No one held a gun to my head. I knew what I was getting into. I had stood in line for this roller coaster. That's when I realized I had two choices. I could grab my kids, throw them in the car, and drive as fast and as far away as I could get from this madness—that thought only brought anxiety and despair. Or I could go back to the table, back to my life, back to my entrepreneur, and hang on tight and enjoy the ride—and that's precisely what I did.

Things never did slow down until cancer struck, and our lives became a full-time staycation, and Phil finally discovered the huge impact of a little word: *no*.

The Chuck-It Bucket

Phil's fragile health forced us to figure out, how do we spend our precious time? How do we simplify our lives? How do we learn to say no? The answer was simple—our core values!

At the numerous Lifepilot workshops we attended over the years, led by our mentor Peter Thomas, we had practiced the principles of aligning our goals with our core values. We had even gone to the workshops with our kids. But now, we were discovering the profound significance these Lifepilot strategies would have in prioritizing our precious time.

Obviously we already knew about the concept of a bucket list. Once Phil got the concept of saying no and was forced to prioritize his activities based on his values, we came up with a "chuck-it" list. In fact, I actually made a "Chuck-It Bucket" that sat on our kitchen counter, and we literally wrote out on paper the things we wanted to chuck and threw them in the bucket.

Here's how it worked. First, we listed our core values, which of course for the Carroll family were the five Fs: family, friends, faith, fitness (health), and finance. As life came at us with choices and opportunities and we were forced to make decisions, we just looked at our list of core values, and if it didn't fall under one of them, it got chucked!

For example, Phil and I traveled the world with the Entrepreneur Organization to various conferences, and when we had the opportunity to go to Istanbul, Turkey, with our business associates, we decided to chuck that opportunity for the first time ever, because Phil's healing and health were more valuable.

We had to chuck going with our son to Moscow to represent Team Canada in an international hockey tournament. That was an excruciatingly painful chuck for Phil. We even chucked some people who were not positive influences in our lives.

We chucked certain shows and movies that were violent and negative because they didn't fit Phil's positive focus in his healing.

Phil eventually had to chuck going to work altogether because he didn't have the energy.

During the years before cancer, I had written a children's book called *Bigsbee's Unbee-lievable Journey to Fly* about the world's first flying bumblebee. It was a metaphorical life skills book for young readers about bee-ginning with a dream, bee-lieving in themselves, bee-ing accepting of others, and ultimately bee-coming all they could be. With Phil's cancer, many sacrifices had to be made. I chucked marketing and promoting my children's book—I put away my dream to focus on my Phil. I also chucked going to Toastmasters, a speaking group I had belonged to for over ten years. Phil's healing was our top priority and value, and our Chuck-It Bucket filled up quickly.

If you had a Chuck-It Bucket:

- What would you chuck?
- What bad habits are getting in the way of being all you can be?
- Are there people in your life who don't share your values or who have a negative impact on you?
- How about the shows or movies you're watching— do they align with your values?

After using the Chuck-It Bucket for a few months, we realized we had learned three incredible life-changing lessons. First, we learned that worry is the biggest waste of time and therefore needs to get chucked, along with fear, uncertainty, and doubt. Those little devils can pop right out of that Chuck-It Bucket over and over and over, so you've got to just keep chucking them right back in. They're poison. They're a misuse of your imagination and a waste of energy.

Second, we learned that when you slow down, time actually slows down, too. I remember one day just sitting outside with Phil, sipping tea, and enjoying our beautiful backyard, when Phil calmly inquired, "What time is it?" I looked at my watch and thought, *Wow, it's only two o'clock!* That was the first time I had ever been surprised by how *early* it was. That's when I had the epiphany: when you do slow down in life, time slows down with you. If worry is a time waster, slowing down is a time *multiplier*.

Third, we learned to never, ever chuck someone you love. Never chuck calling your mother back or watching your son's soccer game or your daughter's dance recital, and never, ever chuck the opportunity to sit in the backyard on an idle Tuesday and watch a hummingbird with the one you love. We had lived in our home on Desert Cove for fifteen years yet never knew we had hummingbirds until we were forced to staycation and pay witness to the remarkable glory of our own backyard. We would sit outside each day watching the magical flying dancers as they fed from our red flower feeder, and we would listen to their humming as if it were the whispers of God spreading a message of hope and time standing still. I am forever grateful we never chucked those precious moments with our hummingbirds.

Another great thing about the Chuck-It Bucket is that it works both ways. What goes in can also come out. At one point as Phil's cancierge, I felt like something was missing in my life. I actually went rummaging through the Chuck-It Bucket to see if maybe I'd chucked something I shouldn't have. I discovered that I had. I had chucked my voice. I had chucked Chats Toastmasters, something that I loved and valued. For over a decade, it had been a nurturing place where I could laugh and cry and learn and share and discover my voice and help others discover theirs. My Chats family was part of my community, part of who I was. I was a connector, an influencer, a teacher, and that part of me was shut down when I chucked my Toastmasters speaking.

Do you know what I did? I actually added "my voice" to our list of values (or rather, my "Foice," as my sixth F), and I started going back to Toastmasters. Thank goodness I did, because now I'm speaking around the world, sharing our stories—engaging my audience with laughter, moving them to tears, inspiring action to better their years—using the skills that I learned and continue to learn at Toastmasters.

I also discovered there was no time limit to pulling something out of the Chuck-It Bucket. I had used the Chuck-It Bucket principle without realizing it when I chucked my broadcasting career to become Phil's wife and raise his children. I never regretted that decision, but that didn't change the fact that broadcasting and documenting others' stories is in my DNA. So for the next twenty-two years, I used these passions to produce elaborate videos for friends' and families' birthday parties, and thick photobooks documenting every year of my children's lives.

During Phil's illness, one day we were looking at Kris Carr's blog *Crazy Sexy Cancer*. That's when I made another discovery: everyone kept asking how we were doing. We could start a video blog called *Following Phil*, where I would document his cancer journey week by week. When we finally beat this thing, we would travel the world sharing his story and inspire those on a similar journey. (You can view this blog at www.JenniferLCarroll.com.)

Today, I'm traveling around the world sharing Phil's story. In the same way Phil was an entrepreneur and did deals until his dying breath, I am a storyteller, and I want to tell stories that can change lives for the better.

I had thought I was chucking my broadcasting career, but really I was taking it to a whole new level. So always remember: you can chuck something temporarily and pick it back up whenever the time is right. You can't deny what you're meant to do!

Celebrate Your Victories

After all the effort you put into hitting a major goal, it's important that you celebrate your success with the team. I always buy something special for myself, like throw a big party. You must have fun, and we do.

Phil Carroll, *The Power of Focus*

Phil knew when to shift his focus from work to celebration. After the closing of every deal, we would put on a huge soirée. We'd invite all of our business associates and friends and family and celebrate every victory, even the smallest ones. When it came to Phil's battle with cancer, he always rallied and found the energy and effort to celebrate life with the people he loved.

Phil spent two months in the hospital fighting for his life, and when he was released, we drove straight to the Phoenix Coyotes' prospect camp, where Austin had been invited to showcase his hockey talents. Ever since he was six years old lying in bed at night staring at the life-size poster of Jerome Iginla, Austin had been dreaming about playing for the NHL, and this was his chance. And so, even though Phil was too weak to stand, jacked up on morphine, and hooked to an oxygen tank in a wheelchair, he was not going to miss celebrating his son's victory.

Not too long after that was Halloween, which is also our daughter Jessica's birthday. Every year since she was a little baby, we have always made Halloween a big deal and dressed up in celebration of her birthday. But this October 31, 2012, our birthday celebration was a bit more solemn than usual. My parents were with us, we had a cake, Jessica opened a few presents, and then she started reading her dad's birthday card, hanging on to every word as if it might be his last.

As things got heavy and emotional, and the waterworks were set to downpour, Phil started his hand-rubbing thing. He looked at me and said, "Jenn, go to our costume closet and grab some costumes. We are not letting one Halloween slip by without the Carrolls doing it up." I grabbed some pirate costumes for my mom and dad, Jessica threw on a dreadlock wig, I put on my Cruella De Vil black-and-white Dalmatian coat and boa, and Phil transformed into a bright yellow bumblebee. We celebrated Jessica's birthday the way we had done for twenty-one years—Phil Carroll style.

> Do you make a habit of celebrating your victories, no matter how small? Is there a party in your future you need to start planning? What pictures and videos are going to play in the movie of your life? What will your legacy be?

Just days before Phil passed away, when he was so weak— at that point he weighed as much as I did—the doorbell rang. Phil's partner Dave, Brenda and her husband Gordy from Three Buoys Houseboats, and friend Danny Nasser were at the door for a surprise visit. Of course, Phil rallied. It took a while, but we got him out of bed, got him dressed, and got his oxygen tank all hooked up. Then Phil had Dave and Danny go to the garage and pull down a dusty old box of magazine and newspaper articles from back in their Three Buoys days.

They sat outside in the backyard, along with Phil's mom, Dolores, and his aunt Gwen, a registered nurse and angel who took a leave of absence to help me take care of Phil. Together they reminisced and laughed and celebrated those past victories. A few days later, Phil was gone. One of the last things he ever did was celebrate his life with the people he loved.

If you ask a successful entrepreneur if they knew exactly how they were going to achieve their success, they'd probably say, "No, but I just knew I was going to get there."

Phil pursued his healing with the same kind of focus he pursued his businesses. He picked his field, which was buying time, and stuck with it. Healing. Living. He stuck to his values by chucking anything that wasn't going to get him closer to that goal of living, of being invincible. And he celebrated every victory, right up to the last days of his life.

Celebrate your victories. Stay focused. Be invincible.

PHIL-OSOPHY #3

Just Keep Swimming

||||||||||||||||||||||||||||||||||

The Carrolls have always loved animated movies, and our absolute family favorite was *Finding Nemo*. We were those parents who would turn on *Finding Nemo* for our kids, and when they got distracted or bored and took off after any "bright shiny thing," we would keep watching. Sometimes I think they write animated movies more for adults than for kids.

If you haven't seen *Finding Nemo*, it's about Marlin, a father clownfish, and his sidekick Dory, who together set out across the ocean to Sydney Harbor on a quest to find Marlin's lost son, Nemo. Marlin has a "glass half empty" perspective and sees danger and despair at every turn. But Dory, a perpetual optimist, always manages to find the fun in their adventure. When things appear bleak she simply breaks into song, "Just keep swimming, just keep swimming!"

At one point on their tumultuous journey, Marlin and Dory meet up with a huge whale. Dory claims she can speak "whale" and goes on to tell the whale their story. Without a comment, the whale swallows them. Not surprisingly, Marlin gives up hope that he'll ever see Nemo again. Yet the ever-optimistic Dory, despite all evidence to the contrary, is sure everything is going to be all right. As it turns out, instead of digesting them, the whale felt compassion for them and was transporting them straight to Sydney. Just when they're certain they're about to be whale lunch, the whale shoots the two little fish out of his blowhole, and they land right in Sydney Harbor.

Maybe you can relate. On your journey—whether you're searching for your son, your long-lost lover, your career, your future, or yourself—have you ever felt as if you've been swallowed by a huge whale? Surrounded by ribs and stomach acid and dead carcasses, you think, "I'm in a freakin' *whale*. This is it. It's done!"

Well, I can relate, and so could Phil. Just like Marlin and Dory, we had to find a way to "just keep swimming," even when all seemed lost. We had to dig a little deeper and find that song inside us.

Phil had always been an athlete. He ran triathlons and marathons, was a heli-skier, lifted huge weights, and had an incredible physique. In every aspect of his life, he was a go-getter. Jessica called him the Energizer Bunny; he just kept going.

I'll never forget—sometimes, before I even got out of bed, Dad would race into my room, clap his hands together, rub them furiously, and ask, "Jess, what kind of day are you going to have today?" Barely awake,

I'd open one eye and say, "Dad, we're going to have a great day," and literally from that moment on, Dad would tackle the day with enthusiasm.

I used to dance after school six days a week; I was doing ballet, tap dance, hip-hop, you name it. One day I came home after pointe class, and my big toes were bleeding. I ran into Dad's arms crying and said, "Dad, I don't know if I like dance any more. I have no life, the girls are bullying me, and I'm still in the back row. I just don't want to do it anymore." Dad said, "Jess, the Carrolls don't give up. You are a dancer. You were born to perform in front of others."

Then Dad came up with this saying, and before every performance I would have to say it back to him. It was, "Sharp moves, big smiles, perform for thousands." That saying has stuck with me to this day. Actually, on my twenty-first birthday, Dad gave me a necklace with those words engraved on it, and I'll cherish it for the rest of my life. I'm now a YouTube influencer, and I still apply that motto to every single one of my videos. I do sharp moves, I have a big smile, and I try to connect with and influence thousands with my messages.

We always worked out as a family. Phil would play this game that drove us crazy—after we had been running for literally an hour, he would point to a tree and say, "Okay, guys, this is it. We're going to race to that tree: one, two, three—go!" So we'd run and push ourselves as hard as we could to get to that tree. Guess what? The minute we'd get there, Phil would say, "Okay, good job. Now let's go to *that* tree"—pointing to another tree further ahead. We knew that when we got to that tree, there was going to be another tree, and another tree, and so on and so forth. It was relentless. For Phil there was always another tree to race to.

Phil had been that healthy, fit, strong, handsome man until the cancer hit—and then he wasn't. But he always "kept swimming." While he was on chemo, he hired a trainer to walk him through very simple little exercises that helped him with his core stability, his balance, and his memory. No matter how Phil was feeling, three times a week Adam would show up, and Phil would pull himself out of his bed and walk into our workout room with his oxygen tank close behind him. He worked out for just fifteen or twenty minutes, but he would do it relentlessly.

This man, who once lived large, eventually saw his world of infinite possibilities shrink down to the size of his house. Towards the end, part of his fitness routine was simply to walk around the yard without his oxygen tank. He started with walking to the rock in our yard and back. Then the next day he walked a little farther to the lemon tree and back. Then, on a good day, he could walk all the way around our property and back. They were small victories, but he just kept swimming.

Two-Pound Weights

Each morning during this time, Phil would sit outside and enjoy his favorite breakfast cuisine: granola and fresh berries, topped with a sprinkle of ground flaxseed. He loved his mornings, sitting in our beautiful Zen-garden backyard in Scottsdale, Arizona, watching the hummingbirds. One morning, as I cleaned up after breakfast, I saw him sitting motionless, staring out into the yard. This once big, burly, fit, athletic, muscular man now sat in a chair that engulfed his small, frail body. I found myself wondering, what does he think about when he's alone? Does he worry, is he afraid, is he praying?

Then I saw one of the most remarkable things I've ever witnessed. Phil reached down into the side of his chair and pulled out one of my little, pink two-pound weights. Not knowing I was watching, with great effort, he lifted that two-pound weight over his head very slowly and slowly brought it down again. Then, with his other arm, he lifted another two-pound weight from the other side of the seat cushion, just as slowly, over his head, and brought it down. Then he did it again, each time sucking in another huge gasp of air from his oxygen tank, struggling to lift those tiny weights with the arms that used to wrap around me, big and muscular and powerful.

I just watched in absolute awe. All the successful businesses he'd created, all of the races he ran, all of the adventures we went on, all of the incredible things this man had done in his life paled in comparison to that moment as I watched my dying husband lift two-pound weights all by himself, with no trainer to motivate him. Just sitting there, taking baby steps towards getting better, relying solely on his will to move and live. Even though he was riddled with cancer in his skull and his bones and his hips and his lungs, poisoned by the chemo fighting to destroy all those cancer cells, he was not going to stop fighting. He was going to just keep swimming.

That moment when you feel like you're in the belly of the whale—it happened a lot when Phil was fighting cancer; it's happening a lot more since Phil passed away. Some moments feel so dark and so hopeless as we try to get by, day by day, without Phil. Then we think about those two-pound weights. In fact, we kept those weights on the kitchen counter for almost a year after Phil passed away, just as a reminder to keep swimming. That no matter what life throws at you, you can still lift a two-pound weight over your head. You can still do something to move forward, whether you call it swimming, fighting for what you believe in, staying focused on your dream, visualizing your future, or just *living*. Those can be some of the most powerful moments in your story.

Two Steps Forward, One Step Back

Phil and I were fortunate enough to meet and befriend an extraordinary man named Nando Parrado, one of the survivors of a 1972 plane crash into the Andes Mountains. The plane was carrying a Uruguay rugby team and more than a quarter of the passengers died, including Nando's mother and sister. Miraculously, seventy-two days later, sixteen survivors were rescued—because of the brave efforts of Nando Parrado, who, together with teammate Roberto Canessa, trekked for a grueling ten days across the Andes with no food or water. We met Nando during the filming of the movie *Alive,* starring Ethan Hawke, in the Canadian Rocky Mountains, close to where we lived at the time. He was a fascinating man, and we bonded with him and kept in touch over the years.

I remember talking to him one night about his survival experience, and he shared some personal stories that were just gut wrenching. For instance, during their ordeal, he noticed that every boy who wrote a letter to someone he loved would die within twenty-four hours, so he decided he would not write a letter. He was going to look his father in the eyes and tell him he loved him in person.

He also talked about how they found two boxes of chocolate-covered peanuts, and each of them was given one peanut that would have to last an entire day. In the morning, they would just lick off the chocolate. In the afternoon, for lunch, they'd chew on half the peanut. Then at the end of the day, they would finish the other half—and that's how they ended up surviving on one chocolate-covered peanut a day.

Nando's most remarkable story was when, after being stranded in the mountains for over two months, he realized that they were dying there, so he strapped on insulation from the airplane, bundled himself up, and decided to go for it—to make an effort to survive. He took off with teammate Roberto Canessa into the Andes. As their journey dragged on, Nando said that as long as he was able to lift a foot and see that foot print in the snow in front of him, he knew he was still alive. He walked for ten days, watching one foot plant in front of the other, one after another after another. Then one miraculous moment, his foot landed on grass rather than snow—and that's when he knew they were saved. Where there was grass, there was water, and where there was water, there was civilization. Not only was Nando saved, the rest of his sixteen surviving teammates were, too.

The next time I saw Nando he was speaking at an Entrepreneur Organization event in Arizona, when Phil was terribly sick. After his speech, I went up to him and told him tearfully about Phil's battle with cancer. About how he was bedridden and fighting for his life, yet he never stopped fighting and putting one foot in front of the other.

Nando just held me as I wept in his arms. I asked, "How do we escape our Andes?" Without a word, he found a piece of paper and wrote this note: "To Phil . . . never give up!! Love is the opposite of suffering. Live long, live for them. We all have our own Andes sometimes in life, but you'll pull through. A big hug, Nando."

Phil always said his cancer was a lot like two steps forward, one step back. Once during chemotherapy, just when he had finally built himself up so he could walk to the neighborhood bridge and back, he got hit with a fever and was in the hospital for a blood transfusion. Lying in the hospital bed, with the bag of blood dripping "B positive" into his veins, he told us, "I guess the lesson of the month is two steps forward, one step back—I guess that's what life's like. I have to keep my faith—I have to keep my faith during this challenging time."

Maybe you're facing a challenge like Nando or Phil was, where you need to focus on simply taking one step at a time—two steps forward, and then one step back, and then another two steps forward, and another back. We all have our own Andes to cross. We all have our own form of cancer. We all have our own challenges and even catastrophes we must find the strength and courage to navigate through. That's life. If we want to keep living, we have to keep putting one foot in front of the other, and never give up. That's how to be invincible.

Yellow Sticky Notes

As Phil's cancierge, I often found myself feeling like I was stuck in the Andes—lost, afraid, hopeless. One time, in particular, I remember walking down the hall, bringing Phil's breakfast to his bedroom. It was my second attempt at his perfect eggs—they had to be not too soft, not too hard. We had a big mirror in the hallway, and I stopped for a moment and looked at myself. I barely recognized the woman looking back. I looked like a million miles of bad road: tired and sad—and frightening, to be honest.

For a split second—because I didn't want his eggs to get cold—I stared at myself in the mirror and smiled until I found a smile remotely resembling something genuine and authentic that might possibly bring joy to my dying husband.

Because as much as I felt as if I had been swallowed by a whale or lost in the Andes, I wasn't having to fight for my life. I wasn't the one having to breathe from an oxygen tank. I didn't have to go to chemotherapy. I wasn't throwing up half the meals I ate. I wasn't in pain all the time. I wasn't wasting away from cancer. I realized in that moment that I had a significant purpose, and it wasn't to bring him eggs. It was to go around that corner and bring him sunshine and joy and a beautiful, loving wife. It was to bring him my love that was still unconditional: pure, honest, authentic, and real.

As soon as I walked around the corner to his room, his eyes lit up and he said, "You look like a ray of sunshine. That's who you are. You are my sunshine."

Every single day after that, I knew what my mission was. The way I was going to get out of my whale, my Andes, was to be Phil's sunshine. So you know what I did? I wrote the word "SMILE" with a big smiley face on a yellow sticky note, and I put it on one end of the hallway mirror. Then I made another one just like it for the other end of the hallway—because it was a long hallway, and I didn't want to lose my smile at the end. And for the rest of our journey through cancer, I did my best to be Phil's sunshine—to turn that corner and radiate love and hope and possibility for him, because my love was *not* dying.

Is there a mirror in your world that needs a sticky note? Maybe it needs to say "smile," or "hug my wife," or "throw the football with my son," or "breathe," or "meditate," or "go for a walk." What reminder do you need to be the best you can be, so that you can get out of that whale's belly and find your Nemo? Or escape your Andes and live your dream?

Keep lifting those two-pound weights one at a time and putting one foot in front of the other, just like Phil did. Be invincible and just keep swimming!

PHIL-OSOPHY #4

Live to Give

||||||||||||||||||||||||||||||||

Two thousand years ago, Roman philosopher Pliny the Elder said, "Home is where the heart is." Home was definitely where Phil's heart always was. His entire adult life revolved around homes, starting with his business Three Buoys, where he showed people how to "vacation large" on houseboats. When Three Buoys sailed off into the sunset, Phil then turned his attention to landlocked investment homes, a venture whose tremendous success enabled him to buy a dream home in Arizona for his family. This home was not only where he raised his kids, but would eventually become his Zen palace, his hospice, and the place he would take his last breath.

Phil cherished our summer home in British Columbia on Skaha Lake, where he spent twenty summers with his children creating their most valued memories of living, loving, and laughing together.

If you're an entrepreneur, you're driven to live an abundant and successful life, allowing you to live large and experience the infinite opportunities life has to offer—for yourself and for your family.

But even with all of Phil's unwavering desire for success, he never lost focus on his journey toward significance. They weren't two separate roads for Phil; they were one road that led to a life of lasting legacy.

Which is why, out of all the homes Phil poured his heart into, what truly captured his passion were the homes he built for Mexican families through Homes of Hope.

Homes of Hope

For fifteen years, Phil and our family traveled to Tijuana, Mexico, with Homes of Hope (www.homesofhope.com) to build a home for a homeless family. Since his passing, we have continued to carry his torch—or rather, his hammer. One of the greatest lessons we taught our kids was to live to give—and thanks to Homes of Hope, they began learning that lesson at a very young age.

Phil had a special way of bonding with everyone he met, whether it was the foul-mouthed cabdriver, the elderly guy watching hockey at the bar, the waitress in the crowded restaurant, or the Mexican fathers he helped build houses for. Over the years with Homes of Hope, Phil came to recognize that regardless of skin color, income, education, size, or age, all the fathers he built with in Tijuana had the same underlying commitment: They worked passionately to create a loving, safe, healthy, nurturing, spiritual world where their wives and children could survive and thrive. Despite their differences, they shared the same core values. That's what made them the same.

Our first build with our kids, when Jessica was nine and Austin was six, was for a man named Santiago and his family. On our last workday, I remember giving Austin a bath after a long day of painting not only the house but himself. As he formed the shampoo suds into another crazy Mohawk hairdo, out of the blue he proclaimed, "Mom, when Dad gets old, I'm going to always take care of him, you know."

I looked at him with the half-bottle of suds piled on his head and supportively replied, "Ah, that's great, Aust." Then I asked curiously, "So, why do you think you need to take care of Dad?"

He plunged his head into the water, dissolving his latest hairdo, and as he wiped the suds off his face, he answered, "Santiago told me today that I'm the luckiest kid alive, 'cause Dad takes such good care of me and gives me so much stuff, and that one day, when he's old, I have to take care of him."

I could just picture Santiago, the fifty-year-old, leathery-skinned, hardworking Mexican man, with his huge hands that had worked tirelessly his whole life. Despite his burly exterior, his eyes reflected a kindness borne from hardship and challenge like nothing my six-year-old son could ever imagine. In his big straw hat, he would have towered over Austin as he shared his wisdom in his broken English with the young child whose father had just helped build his family a home. A home with beds, with a concrete floor, with an actual roof that would not leak—three luxuries Santiago had never had in his fifty years. For the first time in his life, in the morning he would wake up after sleeping on an actual mattress and step onto a concrete floor. When it rained and stormed outside, it would no longer rain or storm inside. Life for Santiago and his family would be changed forever.

When Santiago's home was finished and the keys passed to the family, Austin watched as his dad took off his running shoes and handed them to Santiago. Santiago took off his holey boots, put on Phil's pair of brand new Nikes, and stared down at his feet, bursting with pride. Then Phil, without hesitation, pulled on Santiago's boots, laced them up, gave him a big hug, and said, "I'm going to come back, and we're going to have a barbecued steak together and celebrate your house." It was a profound experience, not just for Santiago and his family, but for our children and for Phil and me.

As we drove away, Jessica said, "Dad, when it feels so good to give, why don't more people do it?" That question resonated with us deeply, and it's what empowers us to return every year to build Homes of Hope.

A few months after that first build, I remember going to a meet-the-teacher event at Austin's school. Austin was in first grade and not really into school like his big sister was, but he was a smart kid nonetheless. I introduced myself to the teacher as Austin Carroll's mom, and her reaction was troubling, to say the least. Tears started to pool in her eyes, and all I could think was, *Oh no, what did he do?*

Without a word, she walked over to a table and opened a folder. She handed me a piece of paper, and on it were the words, "If I had $100, I would . . . " Then there were some lines on which Austin had scribbled, barely legibly, "I wud biy klos and gif it to the por pepul."

Under the words he had drawn several stick people handing clothes to other stick people with big smiles on their faces, and in the background he had drawn a Home of Hope with a crooked roof.

His teacher, choking on the words, said, "This is very special. I didn't give the kids any guidance when it came to this exercise. Most of the students wanted bikes and trips to Disneyland, to go to the moon and to drive a race car, but Austin wanted to buy clothes to give to the poor people in first grade at Quarry Lane Elementary School." Now, that's significant!

Walk Your Talk

The next year when we returned to Tijuana for a new build, Phil didn't forget about Santiago. Sean Lambert, the founder of Homes of Hope and one of Phil's best friends, told us later that after he heard Phil promise Santiago he'd bring him a steak dinner to celebrate, he had thought, *Sure. Everybody says they're coming back and no one does.* But as Sean puts it, "Phil walked his talk and did what he promised—he came back."

Now, there are no addresses where the families we build for live, no street names or house numbers. It's Tijuana's shantytown, but Phil was determined to meet with his building buddy once again and share a steak dinner. One day, he rallied the kids and me, and we headed to Walmart with a Homes of Hope driver and translator to pick up groceries, toys, cleaning supplies, a small portable barbeque—oh, and a few beers for Phil.

I remember winding through the dusty streets of the Tijuana neighborhood, searching for the house Phil and Santiago had built the year before. We were looking for a needle in a haystack! If we did find the house, we had no way of knowing if the family would even be home because there was no way to communicate with them.

The homes were literally stacked on top of each other as we meandered down the horribly rutted gravel roads that led deep into the valley. Relentlessly we searched, until we eventually found our Home of Hope nestled in the side of the hill. But the discovery was anticlimactic— Santiago and his family were nowhere to be seen. So we waited . . . and we waited.

As the sun started to set, Phil and Austin set up the barbecue with the coals, while I marinated the steaks in Ziploc bags with Lea and Perrins and barbeque sauce and Jess wrapped the gifts. Then from the crest of the hill, at the end of the long, potholed dirt road, some figures appeared in the distance. Santiago and his family were coming home, and we were there to greet them. We had a Christmas celebration in July as we unpacked bags of groceries and watched the young Hispanic girls open presents filled with toys and dolls. Phil sat down for the long-awaited steak dinner with his Mexican compadre, and they toasted with bilingual smiles and slightly warm beer. It was one of the best Fourth of July Christmas celebrations ever.

"Phil did everything that way," said Sean. "He did it BIG. This guy had such tremendous energy. Over one hundred thousand people have built with Homes of Hope, and this is the truth— no one encouraged me more than Phil. No one put more energy into saying, 'You're doing a good job, Sean. Keep going. This is awesome. It changed me, and it changed my family.' Phil was the most encouraging person in my life."

Even as Phil's energy faded, his "live to give" legacy grew brighter still. Towards the end of Phil's life, Sean Lambert came to our home to visit Phil, knowing his time was short.

He recalls:

We just sat around the pool. Even though it was a sad

moment, it was a happy moment too, because we read out of John 14.

"Don't let your hearts be troubled. Believe in God. Believe in me. My father's house has many rooms. If it were not so, I would not have told you I'm going there to create a place for you. I will come back and take you with me to be there, so that you can be where I am."

I looked at Phil, and I said, "Jesus is the ultimate Homes of Hope builder, and no one loves Homes of Hope more than Jesus himself, because Jesus is a builder." Then I said, "God is preparing a place for you and for all of us."

Phil got there far too early, quicker than the rest of us, quicker than we all wanted.

The Phil Carroll Pavilion

At the end of Phil's life, on a day that would be his last, something remarkable happened. The doorbell rang. At the door stood Dave and Barb Bamber, our longtime friends from Calgary, along with six other members of the Entrepreneur Organization. They had flown in spontaneously to see Phil. Dave explained that if Phil wasn't up to seeing them, they would understand, but they had something they wanted to share with him that was significant.

Phil welcomed them in. I helped him put on a nice, collared shirt that barely fit him anymore in his frail state. He sat in his huge leather armchair, which he used to fill up but now engulfed him, and greeted these friends from his past. They laughed and shared old stories, and then one of his friends, Phil Sprung, took out a large architectural drawing of his latest project. His company built enormous canvas structures all over the world. He was building one of his Sprung structures on the Homes of Hope campus outside of Tijuana, Mexico. He wanted to name it the Phil Carroll Pavilion, in honor of Phil, for the passion and effort he put into Homes of Hope. Phil Sprung had even superimposed a picture of my Phil's pink 1960 Cadillac El Dorado parked in front of the pavilion. Not something you see every day in Tijuana!

Phil's passion for Homes of Hope and living to give rippled out beyond the circle of our family to impact all the people he knew and loved. Not only did Phil get all of his EO forum members building with Homes of Hope, he also recruited his friends from Vancouver and Arizona. Even his thoracic surgeon, Dr. Elbert Kuo, started building with Homes of Hope.

I find it remarkable and profound that at the end of Phil's life, a life of tremendous success—business success, family success, marriage success, friendship success, abundance, travel, adventure—he was being honored for his generosity and *living to give*.

Phil fell asleep that night, on December 13, 2012, with a picture of the Phil Carroll Pavilion sitting by his bed. He was proud. He was honored. More than just successful, he felt *significant*. The next morning, Phil's life here on earth ended, but his legacy of living to give will live on forever. In that way, he was truly invincible.

Is there a need in the world where your efforts can make a difference? It's just a matter of looking beyond yourself and seeing what's right in front of you. If you look hard enough, you will find that place where you too can give. Try it, and I promise, you'll receive so much more in return. That's how *you* can be truly invincible.

There's a symbolic story about a young boy who's throwing starfish from the beach back into the ocean. There'd been a storm the night before, and all these starfish had washed up on the beach. An old man saw the young boy, walked over, and said, "Son, what are you doing? There's too many starfish; you can't possibly make a difference." The little boy picked up another one, threw it out into the water, and said, "I made a difference to that one." Giving is all about making a difference for one person or family at a time.

If home is where the heart is, where does your heart live? Where will your pavilion be built once you are gone? Let your giving become a valued part of your story, and make you truly invincible.

Leave No Words Unspoken

||||||||||||||||||||||||||||||||||

Phil always had his own way with words. Despite the fact that he was educated and brilliant, he never fully grasped the English language in all its complexity. To be honest, he often massacred it with mispronunciations that came to be known as Phil-isms. After he would order his favorite breakfast of eggs Benedict, as the waiter was walking away, Phil would often call out, "Hey, don't forget the extra holiday sauce!" We always got a good laugh out of that one. But despite our laughter and suggested corrections, Phil never really did see the difference between *hollandaise* and *holiday*. To him, those were just minor details, and he never got bogged down in details. He was the "big picture" guy.

His business partner Dave recalled the time when Phil came blasting into the office after a morning golf game with a prospective new salesman and announced, "He's our guy!"

"How do you know for sure, Phil?" Dave inquired.

Phil answered, "You can discover more about a person in an hour of play than in a year of conversation."

Dave was thoroughly impressed by the insight and asked Phil who he was quoting. With great confidence, Phil replied, "Pluto."

"I think he's a Disney character, Phil," Dave said with a grin. Phil shrugged his shoulders, blew it off, and never stopped quoting his favorite philosopher, Pluto!

Phil also loved music. Whenever one of Phil's favorite songs came on, he would sing along as loud as he could, whether he was in the car, the shower, the back of the boat, a crowded dance floor, or lying out by the pool. Yet he knew surprisingly few of the actual lyrics. Instead, he just made up his own version and belted out the Phil-icized rendition with great confidence and somewhat painful pitch. Once again, the exact words were mere details. Bottom line, Phil loved words, even though he rarely got them right according to *Webster's Dictionary* or an album's liner notes.

His slightly limited mastery of the English language never stopped him from expressing his gratitude in an avalanche of cards, letters, and notes. Here's one of the hundreds of love letters he wrote to me.

Love letter from Phil to Jennifer, June 23, 2010 (our anniversary):

Look at the beautiful girl I married. Wow! What a lucky guy. Our story, how we met in the shower, our trip around the world . . . it's a romance novel. God blessed us with this exciting journey. I love your kisses, hugs, laughter, energy, athleticism, spirit, kindness, thoughtfulness, parenthood, wisdom, and how humble you are. You have masterminded our children's upbringing, and they are now sailing into the future with confidence. You should be proud of all the wonderful memories and accomplishments over the last twenty years. I am blessed and grateful for how I feel today about you and our marriage. God bless you, and I love you.

With passion,
Phil

Words Matter

Even though he didn't get hung up on grammatical details, Phil knew that words matter. Words change lives. A few simple words, when strung together in a certain order, can profoundly alter our entire life in an instant. Words like, "You're pregnant." "I do." "The helicopter never came back." "It's a hockey player!" "You have cancer."

In May 2012, Jessica, Austin, Dave Steele, close friend Neil Balter, and I were brought into a private room at St. Joseph's Hospital in Phoenix, Arizona. Dr. Elbert Kuo, Phil's kind, skilled doctor spoke to us and said the words, "Phil has two weeks to live." Dr. Kuo explained, while we sat speechless, that Phil's prostate cancer had somehow morphed into another completely different form of cancer, and it had invaded his lungs. Phil was not only battling prostate cancer, but lung cancer, and it was the lung cancer that was about to take his life.

His doctors later told us that Phil's prostate cancer was one of the most aggressive cancers they had seen. Apparently it's very unusual for prostate cancer to transform this way. We weren't really surprised to hear this. Of *course* Phil's cancer would be an overachieving disease.

Phil would undergo more than twenty surgeries in the next several weeks. The goal was to implode the baseball-sized mass of cancer in his lungs that was slowly taking his voice, his breath, and his life.

On the morning of one of his many surgeries, Phil was high as a kite on morphine, waiting to be taken back to the OR. After a brief prayer, Phil started belting out his favorite Nickelback song, "Rock Star": "I want to be Elvis without the hassles . . . I want a bleached blonde at the Playboy mansion . . . Drug dealer on speed dial . . . Hey, hey, I want to be a rock star!" As usual, it was his Phil-icized version.

I told him, "You're always going to be my rock star. Go rock this surgery!" As the nurses wheeled him away, I could still hear him repeating the chorus, "I want to be a rock star!"

I Died!

"I died, I died!" Phil exclaimed in his raspy, post-op voice. He had made it through his "rock star" surgery, and he looked like he had seen the ghost of Elvis himself. He yelled out again, painfully, "I died!" He was trembling as he explained to Jessica and me what he had experienced.

He said he had been underwater, looking up onto a dock filled with all of his friends and family: his mom and dad, his sister Lisa, and his friends Scott, Dave, Neil, and Gary. They were reaching down into the water towards him, and he was struggling to grab hold of their hands. But something was pulling him deeper and deeper into the watery abyss. He could see Jess and me calling to him, pleading that he come back. Just as he was about to give up and he thought he was gone, a strong hand reached down, grabbed his forearm, and pulled him up. It was his son. Although he never saw his face, he somehow knew it was Austin who had pulled him out of death's grip.

He gasped for breath as we all sat looking on helplessly. It seemed so surreal. Was it the morphine talking? Had he had a near-death experience? It was all so confusing. Still, we felt so grateful that he was here with us, struggling for breath, fighting for his life, trying to hold on.

The doctors explained that Phil had an intubation tube down his throat that physically allowed him to breath during the operation. Once he was alert, they removed it, and for a few seconds there's often a sensation that might feel like you can't breathe. When that happened to Phil, he panicked and started grabbing at the nurse, which prolonged the removal process, and at that point, according to the doctors, he had most likely hallucinated from the morphine. Here's how Jessica described her dad's frightening experience in her blog.

"I died. Jess, I died. I died. Please give me your strength. I died. I need you." The first time I saw my dad in the hospital that day, those were the words that came out of his mouth. I missed the "What's up, Scrubber? What kind of day are you going to have today?" and my answer, "A great day, Dad."

I decided to spend that night with Mom at the hospital. No words could describe this experience. It was a night from hell. Dad was up every fifteen minutes— coughing, yelling, throwing ice, throwing his water, wanting more water, wanting more drugs, having to

*go to the bathroom, wanting us to scratch his back,
pulling his tube out of his body, angry. He kept asking,
"What's going on? What's next? I don't get it. This
system doesn't work. I want to figure it out. What am I
supposed to do now?"*

*I could tell my father was lost, wanting to regain
control over his life.*

Father's Day

Father's Day happened to fall during those four weeks at the
hospital with Phil. The kids bravely fought back their emotions,
or at least tried to, wrote Father's Day cards for their dad, and
read them to him out loud as they celebrated the most significant
Father's Day of their lives.

Jessica wrote (at age twenty-one):

*Dad, thank you for being my number one dad. The other
day, you asked me what I see when I look at you. I see
a proud man, a remarkable father, a loving husband,
my best buddy, a positive go-getter, and a warrior. You
overcome obstacles and challenges by making the right
decisions, being proactive, appreciating the support
from your loved ones, seeking help, and only focusing
on the positive side.*

*You are the first man I ever loved. I would not be the
woman I am today, at this stage in my life, if it weren't
for you—the lessons you taught me, your love, your
positivity, your energy, and your motivation. One word
to describe you is unbelievable. Looking back on my*

life, we have shared some unforgettable and incredible memories.

- *Surfing in Okanagan Falls with my girlfriends*

- *Laughing our guts out while watching* The Hangover

- *Blasting down Lake Louise ski hill on our snowboards and, of course, grabbing a beer after*

- *Seeing my number one fan sitting in the audience, never missing a dance recital, football game, or pep rally*

- *Building numerous homes for the Homes of Hope*

- *But most of all, scuba diving. Diving down with you is a moment I will always remember. A true daddy-daughter moment.*

There is something about you that brings confidence, energy, and determination into people's lives. You have always been the fearless leader of your friends and family, and now it is our turn to be your fearless leader. When I look around the waiting room, I see your friends and family full of hope, faith, and love. The waiting room should be named Phil Carroll's Room. Dad, I will always love you unconditionally, and just as you taught me, I will never give up.

Life has its ups and downs and everything in between, but just know that I am your number one cheerleader. I will always be your little girl to laugh with, surf with, and dance with. Just as I am your cheerleader, I know that you are my number one fan. As Dory would say, "Just keep swimming," Dad. There is always a light at the end of the tunnel, and your tunnel is filled with love, faith, and optimism.

Love you forever and always,

Your Little Scrubber,
Jessica

Austin wrote (at age eighteen):

Happy Father's Day to the strongest, most empowering, and inspirational person I know. I may have wanted to rip your head off at times, but I thank you for all of your tough-love chats and motivational speeches, because as much as it seemed I didn't listen, your encouragement and ability to motivate me is what has allowed me to have success in life.

Our memories are endless. I have never had more fun with a single person as I've had with you. All of your Phil-isms, goofy ties, and your famous "I-don't-give-a-bleep" swagger brings so much laughter and joy to the lives of everyone around you.

Recently, everyone has been talking about hope. Hope

is a feeling that what is wanted can be had. Dad, all my life, you have instilled hope into me. You've made me feel that anything I wanted I could have if I put enough hope into achieving it. Hope to make the big team, hope to get drafted, hope to clear the wake. If there is one thing you taught me, it's to never lose hope. I'm not stopping now.

I have never regretted a moment with you. Every memorable moment I have had in life has been with you. I have yet to see a father and son with a better relationship than you and I have. You push me, and I need to be pushed. You chill with me when the time is right. You are my bro and forever my best friend. You are always so strong for me and our family, but now it is time for us to be strong for you. I will always be here, and I love you no matter what. You are a picture-perfect dad and a picture-perfect person.

Love you bro,
Austin

Phil smiled and laughed as his kids shared these magical words. Suddenly a curtain swung open at the side of the room. It was a young nurse who had found herself trapped in the corner while preparing some medications for Phil when the letter reading started.

In an effort to not interrupt, she decided to wait it out and listen. As she came out from behind the curtain, she was blowing her nose and wiping her eyes. After just standing speechless for a moment, she said, "I've never been touched more by such words of love to a father." She said to Phil, "The love your children have for you is remarkable." Then she thanked us for accidentally allowing her to share in our special Father's Day moment.

Morphine Talk

While Phil was in the hospital, he was jacked up on morphine 24/7 to help him though the pain of all those surgeries. Let me tell you, as horrible, serious, and dire as his situation was, Phil, as always, was blasting out humor left, right, and center—albeit unintentionally—with his morphine talk. My favorite morphine story also happened on Father's Day when Austin was alone with Phil in his room. Suddenly, Phil said, "Austin, go tell the nurse to get me more LSD." Austin looked at Phil in disbelief, not sure if Dad really meant what he said, so he tried to clarify.

"LSD?"

"Yes, yes, I need some more LSD."

Poor Austin, who does what his father tells him to do 99.9 percent of the time, obediently walked over to the nurse, who had just finished blowing her nose after the Father's Day card incident, and quietly whispered, "My dad would like some more LSD." Now, deep in the back of his brain, something was telling him, *I don't think they give out LSD at hospitals. Isn't it a street drug? But maybe under circumstances like Dad's, they give it out to him like morphine to help control the pain.*

That little voice inside of his head was (mostly) right, and the nurse chuckled loudly, thinking that Austin was kidding, which embarrassed him even more. The nurse informed Austin that they don't give out LSD at hospitals and that maybe she should come in and see what Phil really wanted. Sure enough, Phil announced to the nurse, "I want some more LSD," as he pointed to the counter where there was a bottle of Listerine on its side, obviously empty. Phil-isms on morphine can be a dangerous thing!

After thirty challenging days, twenty different surgeries, daily X-rays and MRIs, a constant morphine drip, round-the-clock care, his family literally camping out in the ICU waiting room, and getting to know all the nurses and doctors on a first-name basis, Phil had a breakthrough. The tumor did implode, and it was dissolving. He was physically coughing up the huge tumor, one cough at a time. He was getting better. He was getting stronger. He was breathing.

All of a sudden, the prognosis of two weeks to live evaporated. He did not drown in that hospital. Thanks to the doctors, the surgeries, the morphine, and the support of his family and friends, Phil became a lung cancer survivor. If Phil had only had lung cancer, he would still be alive today.

Speechless

Phil got so strong that we were able to get him on a privately chartered airplane, thanks to our dear brother-in-law Ron Mathison. We flew up to Victoria, British Columbia, for three weeks to watch Austin play for the Victoria Royals in the Western Hockey League (WHL). Every day was a challenge. Every minute a struggle. Pain, meds, sleepless nights—but Phil was able to watch his son live out his dream, and that made all the difference. I remember Phil as he watched Austin's games, and for those few hours, cheering on his boy as he was shooting, passing, back-checking, and even fighting, Phil was his old self again—living large.

When we returned from Victoria, we went to see his doctor. He put up an image of Phil's skeletal system, which was mostly a bright yellow image of his skull, his ribs, his spine, and his hip bones. Scattered throughout the yellow were black splotches, about fifteen of them.

"So the cancer is here and here and here and here?" I said, as I pointed to the black splotches. The doctor paused and shook his head. I felt a panic flood my body. He said, "I'm sorry to say, the black spots are where there is no cancer. The yellow is where the cancer is."

We were speechless. It was worse than we thought. The prostate cancer was not only still there, it had spread into his bones and his skull. It was all through his ribs and in his hip bones. He was riddled with cancer.

I had been Phil's full-time caregiver for one year. Three months earlier, I had been told he had only two weeks to live. But it was only at that moment I knew that I would soon be a widow. I knew Phil's time was limited to days.

No more words were said. We didn't need them; the image told the horror story in grotesque detail. Phil and I got up, he grabbed my hand as we walked out, and we didn't say one word about dying. We just drove home.

Both our children were busy living their lives. Jessica was in college, finishing up her last month or two of classes. Austin was still up in Victoria playing hockey for the WHL. They too knew their dad's days were limited. At times they wanted to drop out of their courses and teams, come home, and just spend time with their dad. I remember telling them that a huge part of what got us through each day—our One Fun Thing every day—was experiencing our children pursuing their dreams.

The Christmas Card

Austin called me one night, and I could barely make out his words. I thought we had a bad connection, and then I realized he was sobbing so hard he could barely speak. He said, "Mom, I just had this panic attack. What if Dad just died suddenly and he doesn't know how I feel?"

I said, "Austin, Dad knows how you feel. He knows how much you love him. He knows you are his best friend. But here's an idea: It's almost Christmas. You know how much Dad loves cards, so why don't you write him a Christmas card? Tell him how you feel. Maybe write a few little stories about some of your favorite memories with him, like tobogganing in Canada, or playing hockey on the outdoor rink in the backyard, or snowboarding, or playing on the boat in the summer. Share some of those stories." We talked for a while and reminisced about the good times with Dad. I could tell he felt a little better. I hung up.

Sadly, Phil never made it to Christmas like we'd expected. In fact, one week after I got that call from Austin, Phil passed away of complications from prostate cancer. I've been asked many times what it was like to be with my husband, the love of my life, "my person," as he died, as he took his last breath, as he left this world. Was it horrible? Was it a nightmare?

Some of you might have also been with someone you loved on his or her deathbed. For me, it was strangely magical. Kind of like our entire marriage: strange, yet a beautiful miracle. I remember Phil lying on his bed. His mother, his father, his aunt Gwen, our housekeeper Veronica, and I were all surrounding him. He was in a state of shock. He was dying. He was trying to get up. We were trying to calm him.

Phil's mom sat beside him, and they prayed together for a while. Then it was my turn. I sat beside Phil and held his hand. He had little strength, but he was able to look into my eyes, deeper into my eyes than he'd ever looked before, as if he was looking into my soul. As he stared at me, his mouth started to move. He was trying to find words, those special, precious last words that he wanted to share with me. The cancer had spread to his skull, and into his vocal cords. At the end of his life, Phil spoke with barely a whisper. I watched him struggle to form words and find a voice to project them, but he couldn't.

I gently placed my fingers over his beautiful lips and said, "Phil, it's okay. You don't have to say anything. You've said it all. You've left no words unspoken. I know that you love me down to the core of your being, because you told me. You've told me as you looked into my eyes. You've told me in letters. You've told me in love notes. Every morning of my life, you woke up and asked, 'How's my beautiful wife?'

"I know how proud you are of your children, that they continue to move confidently towards their dreams, and that they're living the life that they imagined for themselves. They know how proud you are, because you told them. You told them in words, and in words of tough love, and in letters, and in encouragement. You've told them over and over and over and over. They know."

As I spoke to him, his eyes relaxed. His mouth softened. I could sense peace as his soul surrendered. I went on. I went on for what felt to be an eternity, but it was probably only a few more minutes. I spoke of all the things that he had shared with us, all the words. Then he took in his final breath of life, and let it out so slowly . . . and my Phillip was gone.

If you found yourself on your deathbed, holding the hand of the person you loved the most in the world, and you had words to speak but no voice, could they speak your last, precious words? Or have you left words unspoken?

After Austin called me that one night when he was in such a panic about telling his dad how he felt, he chose not to write a Christmas card. Instead, he wrote a letter, and he emailed it to me that same night. The next morning, after Phil had his morning granola with his berries and flaxseed sprinkled on top, I handed him a two-page love letter from his eighteen-year-old son that read:

I just sat on my bed and flipped through every page of Mom's amazing photo book, 18 Years of Living a Life as Austin Carroll, *and realized that there hasn't been a day in my cherished life that you haven't been a part of. You may not have been with me or even in the same part of the world because of the rock-star life you live, but in some way you have been there. Every speed bump or crossroad I come to in life, I think about everything you have taught me and inspired in me, right from wrong, good ideas or bad, and I think to myself, "What would Big Phil do?"*

Not a day goes by that I don't talk about the legend and hero my father is. You're the single most important person in my life and always will be. The moments and memories we have shared are countless and effortless, because of the unique love and bond we share. It is unlike any boy could dream of, playing on the outdoor hockey rink, going tobogganing at Banff, taking me to the zoo, the hockey camps all across the world, allowing me to spend my summers at Okanagan Falls on the boat, teaching me to snowboard, wakeboard, and ski, bringing hockey into my life, teaching me to skate, score goals, and win championships, teaching me I can achieve anything I set my mind to, and allowing me to live the life any kid could only dream of.

Everything you have ever done for me, or pushed me to do, was for my benefit. Through the good times and tough-love times, you just wanted me to become better. Without that push, I could never have been what I am today. I thank you so much, and I'm lucky to have you as my motivational coach. You have taught me that when the going gets tough, the tough get going, and that the words "I can't" don't exist in my vocabulary.

In my mind, you are invincible. I have never doubted you a second in my life. I wish I could put into words how I feel about you. You are my role model, my best friend.

I love you. I love you. I love you.
Austin

As Phil read that letter, tears streamed down his face. He said, "That is the greatest gift a father could ever get from his children. Words of love and appreciation." Days later, when Phil passed away, no words were left unspoken.

Words matter. Go to your phone and text someone you love. Go to your computer and email someone you love. Write a letter and mail it. Pick up the phone and call someone who needs to hear your unspoken words. Because you don't know when that opportunity may be gone forever. You don't know when the people you love are going to take their last breath, or when you're going to take yours. What do you need to share before that happens? What invincible words will be part of your story?

The Greatest Is Love

||||||||||||||||||||||||||||||||

As you know, on June 23, 1990, Phil and I stood in Saint Mary's Cathedral and vowed to love each other: "To have and to hold, from this day forward, for better, for worse, for richer, for poorer, in sickness and in health, until death do us part." And we did. We loved and honored each other all the days of our lives. At that service, my father, Peter, stood at the pulpit with great reverence, and read 1 Corinthians 13:

> *Love is patient, love is kind. It does not envy, it does not boast, it is not proud. Love never fails. When I became a man, I put the ways of childhood behind me. For now we see only a reflection as in a mirror; then we shall*

see face to face. Now I know in part; then I shall know
fully, even as I am fully known. Now these three remain:
faith, hope, and love. But the greatest of these is love.

Phil unquestionably lived large and loved large. Phil's love
came from his parents, who celebrated their sixty-fifth wedding
anniversary just before he died. It also came from his four siblings,
who loved each other both functionally and dysfunctionally, as
families do. It also came from God; his love for God only grew
after experiencing the tragedies of losing his brother, two sisters,
and three cousins.

In fact, if I were to describe Phil in one word, it would be
passionate—impetuously, impulsively, instinctually passionate. If I
were to describe him with an emoji, it would be a big, red heart.
Our daughter Jessica had a different answer:

If I could describe Dad as an emoji, it would be the
smiley face with the sideways kiss, because when Dad
went in for a kiss, it wasn't a normal kiss. It was a juicy
kiss. He would full-on lick his lips—then go in for the
kiss. I asked him, "Why do you wet your lips so much
before you kiss me?" He said, "I never want my girl to
have a dry kiss from her dad." Dad brought a whole
new meaning to the term "sticky smooch."

His love was so rich because it started with himself. Phil was
Phil's greatest fan. As much as we brag about how amazing he
was, he was a legend in his own mind as well. The first time I met
Phil, at the Special Olympics fundraiser, he was going on and on
about all the amazing things he was doing, and how incredible his
life was, and how incredible the people were in his life. When he

left, I thought, "Well, I certainly won't forget his name, because I definitely had my fill of Phil!" Yes, he was a bit full of himself, but he was just as braggadocious about *all* of his people—his friends, his parents, and—oh, my gosh—his children and his wife. He saw life through those rose-colored glasses.

I've often said that sometimes I wanted to *be* Phil more than I wanted to *have* Phil. That was certainly true when it came to his love for himself. To some it came off as arrogance, self-centeredness, egotism, cockiness, but to the people who knew and loved him, it came off as confidence and a bright light of love for others. I truly believe that Phil's strong belief in himself and his God, his ability to live large, and his love for his family, his people, his puppies, the environment, and giving back came directly from his core of self-love. It allowed him to love others even more passionately and intensely than those who don't love themselves the same way. He personified what the airline attendants tell us to do in case of an emergency: "Before you put the oxygen mask on your loved ones, you must first put it on yourself." We are unable to love or take care of others until we first love and take care of ourselves.

Phil had a huge heart, and with it came a huge life and a great legacy of love. In that way, he was invincible.

> If you truly loved yourself and believed in yourself, how would your life be different? How might your purpose or place in the world change? Could that self-love manifest as a bigger, more fulfilling life?

I've been asked over and over about the greatest lesson I learned during my life with Phil—both when living large as part of his rock-star entrepreneurial life, and living while Phil was dying. I learned that all of the "success" and the "stuff" that matters to us so much when we're young and healthy—climbing the corporate ladder, a big bank account, winning awards, scoring goals, the cars, the watches, the jewelry, the clothes, the number of followers on Instagram—doesn't matter at all when you're facing death. The only thing that matters are "your people," sitting by your bed, holding your hand, looking into your eyes as you find those last, precious words to share and let out your last breath. The people you love. Love is all that matters. Phil always loved deeply and passionately during his life, but as he got closer and closer to his end, he recognized more and more the power of love. That love is *it*. That the greatest of all is love. Love makes us invincible.

Greek Isle Bromance

Phil constantly surrounded himself with people who shared his unique passion and love for life—like his best buddies Dave Steele, Dave Bamber, and Billy Trimble. Immediately after Phil and Dave Steele met Dave Bamber and Billy on a crazy trip to Mexico, they planned a big guys' trip to Europe, where they wreaked havoc through the Greek Isles—and oh, the stories they told.

One of my favorites was when they rented a sixty-foot yacht in Mykonos, Greece, and discovered the stereo speakers were ancient. Phil was all about music, and he certainly knew boats— his houseboats had the best of everything, especially the speakers. Right there in the harbor, Phil went on a mission to find new speakers! Go big or go home! It's not as if there were an electronics store at the marina, but he finally found a small nightclub that hadn't opened yet for the night and bought the guy's speakers right off the wall. Phil paid the nightclub owner twice what he originally paid for them, and the owner himself hauled them to the boat. To the captain's horror, out went the old and in went the brand-new

Big Awesome Speakers from the nightclub. And that was how Phil cruised with his boys through the Mediterranean: large and loud!

When that infamous trip ended, so did their era of bachelorhood, and those four best amigos ended up getting married, reproducing, and spending a lifetime of friendship together.

Each year our four families would all go to Mexico as a group to build with Homes of Hope. We'd spend summers together at a cabin condo complex where we all have property, outside of Kelowna, British Colombia, and we still take a trip together every year to somewhere in this great big world of adventure and opportunity. We've gone on African safaris, dive trips to the Great Barrier Reef in Australia, and cruises and yacht trips in the Caribbean and Mediterranean (always with awesome speakers). We climbed the Great Wall of China, snowboarded the slopes of St. Moritz, Switzerland, and rode camels in Dubai.

Phil always put great effort not only into his business, but also into his relationships. And what you put into anything in life is what you get out. We always cherished our friends, our peeps, as our extended family. For that reason, we've shared our lives with an incredible group of people.

Who are your "peeps"? Who adds value to your life, makes you laugh, helps you find the missing words to the song or the story of your life? Who are those cherished people who make you feel alive and whole and who nurture your soul? Those are your peeps, and theirs is the love that matters. What can you do today to appreciate and nurture those relationships?

Remember to leave no words unspoken, and that love is all that matters in life! That's what it means to be invincible.

If I Had Shot Him When I Wanted To . . .

Phil and I had an extraordinary marriage. It was awesome, but it was not perfect. Phil was definitely not the easiest husband in the world. To be honest, he was bossy—it was always "my way or the highway." He was even a bit of a bully at times. Because I'm amiable, I fell into place, but I sometimes struggled to find my voice and let it be heard. At one point I actually wrote the outline of a book about how to survive and thrive in a long-term relationship with an entrepreneur. I titled it, *If I Shot Him When I Wanted To, I'd Be out of Prison by Now.* I thought the title alone would get me on the Today show for sure.

Here are the three most important chapters:

Chapter 1: "Date Night/Date Flight." Phil, no matter how busy his life got, always made time for me, both when we were dating and when we were married. Every week on our date night, we would go out for dinner or go dancing, and I knew that I would have his undivided attention.

In the early 2000s, Phil was especially focused on business. He had the high-pro glow, that Midas touch, you might say. In his words, he was "making stuff happen." (Except he didn't say "stuff.") Although he was at his best at work, he brought that bossy attitude home, which made him hard to be around a lot of the time. During those times, instead of a date night, we'd have a date "flight." In other words, if we weren't clicking at all, Phil would call and say, "Jenn, I've booked us to go to Venice. Here's our flight; be on that plane. You don't even have to sit beside me." Trust me, there were at least two trips I did not sit beside him. We would get there, discuss the issue and our feelings, and in no time we were like teenagers dating again. We would forget about the petty argument, the misunderstanding, or the bullying that was going on in our real life, and we would disappear and reconnect, just like lovers for the first time.

Chapter 2: "Get a Wife." Not a life, but a wife. Actually, by getting a wife, I got a life. When Phil married me, I was his wife. I took care of him: I did his laundry, I made his meals, I did what he wanted me to do. Eventually I found myself struggling with my self-identity. I had willingly given up my career in broadcasting to raise our kids, but I still wanted to write, I wanted to speak, I wanted to do something that was more purposeful to me than just cooking and cleaning for him. We came up with a solution: Phil hired *me* a wife—or, rather, a nanny. Her name was Suzanne Gallardo. She was from the Philippines, and she was not the nanny to my kids. She was the nanny to my husband. She took great care of him. She cooked all of his meals, she did all of his laundry, she did all of his errands, and I got to do what I love to do. Which was be a great mom to my kids, be a great wife to my husband, and tap into my voice and my own brilliance as a writer, a producer, and a speaker. It was a win-win. Remember, if Mom's happy, everybody's happy! A happy wife means a happy life. Phil grew to appreciate that mantra . . . a lot!

Phil didn't simply hire people; he adopted people. We didn't just employ Susie to take care of Phil's needs—the ironing, cooking, and chores. Phil had a passion for travel, and Susie always came along on our trips to babysit our kids so Phil and I could have some adult play at night. But she didn't just watch the kids—oh, no—Susie went snorkeling with us, took surfing lessons with us, and even went snowskiing with us. Phil was her downhill skiing teacher, and Susie, who had barely seen snow before, gave it her best effort. Phil did the snowplow with her for an entire day. Susie never really picked up the sport, but she had fun getting black-and-blue that day in Whistler.

One day Susie announced that she was pregnant—I was standing before her, two months pregnant myself. We went through our pregnancies together: I delivered my huge Mack truck of a hockey-player son, and two months later she delivered Austin and Jessica's little brother from another mother.

Tragically, Susie developed breast cancer and was given a terminal diagnosis. A year after her son, Ruskin, was born, she went back to the Philippines and passed away. Her husband, Edgar, and one-and-a-half-year-old Ruskin eventually came back to Calgary. Phil and I loved that little boy. We got him into the same school, the same hockey program, and the same gymnastic program as Austin. During the week, while Edgar became established at work, we looked after Ruskin.

I had promised Susie that I would take care of him, and he has become our surrogate son. Phil taught Ruskin how to snowski, waterski, and wakesurf, and Ruskin is truly part of our family. I fondly remember him running up to me after his kindergarten class with Austin and calling me Mom. We made sure he got a full education, and just this year, Ruskin graduated from the University of Calgary.

Although you don't have to adopt the whole family like we did, everyone—including wives—deserves a wife.

Chapter 3: "Recognize the Brilliance in the BS." In other words, the key to a successful relationship with an entrepreneur is to recognize and find humor in each other's differences.

There's a joke about a little boy whose parents thought he was too optimistic, so they took him to a psychologist. In an attempt to bring perspective to his rose-colored world, the psychologist and the parents piled high a whole bunch of horse manure. When they showed the boy this pile, he immediately dove into the middle of it and began digging. "What are you doing?" the psychologist asked. "With all this manure," the little boy replied, beaming, "there must be a pony in here somewhere!"

That boy was Phil. He was the guy who could see the brilliance in all situations. He was the guy who saw the ponies hidden deep inside the horse manure of life.

In my marriage to Phil, I was forced to do the same thing. Because of his type-A, driven-entrepreneur, bull-in-a-china-shop personality, he was going to live his life a certain way. I chose to recognize this "way" as brilliance, and recognize that while he wasn't perfect, neither was I. Diving into the manure and discovering the humor in our differences made all the difference to our marriage.

Phil's Party Bus

One of the saddest days of Phil's cancer journey was also the day I was most frustrated with him. He was adamant that he didn't want anyone to know he had cancer, and I couldn't understand why he wasn't telling his friends. He was about to start chemo and begin this huge ordeal of fighting for his life, and he didn't want to share it with the people he loved? I asked him why, and at first he said he didn't want to worry them. Then he said something that really broke my heart. "Jenn, all my life I've been Fun Phil. The guy that gets everybody on the party bus, the guy that celebrates life, the guy that makes stuff happen. I'm that guy. Fun, healthy Phil." With tears in his eyes, he said to me, "No one will want to be around Sick Phil. No one will be the same when I'm Sick Phil."

I remember looking at him in disbelief: How could he think that? I realized he was working so hard to be loved as this positive, happy, larger-than-life guy. He thought being that guy was what made people love him, and once he stopped being that guy, his people wouldn't love him as much.

He soon came to realize how terribly wrong he was. After Phil found out he had lung cancer and was given two weeks to live, and after one of his twenty-some surgeries to try to save his life, I'll never forget how shocked I was to walk down the hospital hall into the visitors' lounge and be greeted by a dozen people: Dave and Sherry Steele and Billy Trimble, who flew in from Vancouver; our local friends Neil and Lynn Balter, Gary Castrucci, Brent Barker, and Misty and Scott Vogtritter; and my mom and dad, their little Maltese puppy, Mia, and my sister Tara, who flew in from Calgary. They were all there.

That waiting room full of people, our group of gloriously dysfunctional friends and family, set up camp there for the next three weeks. Manning this well-oiled hospitality machine were my besties, Misty Vogtritter and Lynn Balter, who made sure there was round-the-clock food, laughter, music, and well-managed visitors. They trickled in one at a time to see Phil, raise his spirits, and help his healing.

That's when Phil realized that even when he was sick, people still wanted to be on his party bus. Not just for the good times, but to be there with him in the dark times, and with them, they brought the light.

When Phil got home from the hospital, we had a revolving door of people who wanted to visit Phil to encourage him and share fun stories from the old days. Dave Steele, Neil, and Scotty were like the Three Stooges entertaining Phil. Phil's greatest foodie friend, Larry Rosenberg, came to visit with a mission, "Project Phatten Phil," and showed us how to get more calories in Phil to help him fight his battle.

James Fiero came in from London, England, and taught us the importance of alkaline water and juicing. Bridgette cut his hair and made him look like Justin Timberlake, at least in his mind. Our neighbor Jim Osborne brought frozen yogurt to Phil every single night—and sometimes it was the only thing that Phil could keep down. Scotty would take Phil into the pool almost every day, and they would walk their laps together. Danny Nasser from Calgary, Enrique from Switzerland, the Schlosses from LA, and Lori Mottlowitz from Chicago all blasted in to share some good old times and some good old laughs. Billy and Robert Kulhawy came to visit in November, both with mustaches, and Robert let Phil actually take an electric razor and shave off his mustache. What a brave soul, and he did it all in honor of Phil and the Movember movement, creating conversations and awareness about prostate cancer and men's health issues.

Phil was overwhelmed to receive all this love from his people. They brought him support, encouragement, and recognition of how hard he was working to fight this disease. He finally understood that people loved him unconditionally. And it revitalized him. There was no question in Phil's mind, or mine, that their love—their prayers, their laughter, and their tears—is what fed his soul and allowed him to live seven months beyond his prognosis. He spent those seven months not waiting to die, but living every moment, as large as he could.

Good-Bye

Many people came to say good-bye to Phil those last few weeks. One who really touched me was Billy Trimble, who had flown in from Vancouver in November. I remember Phil lying on the couch in the living room and Billy standing in front of Phil, entertaining him. They were laughing about their Greek yacht trip and the infamous speakers, partying, crazy summers getting locked out of apartments naked, and houseboating—one story after another after another. They were laughing and they were crying, and Phil was just beaming with joy as Billy replayed all their glory days.

Eventually Phil got tired, and Billy understood. Still elated from all those funny stories, he said, "Yeah, you rest, Phil," and he kissed Phil on the forehead, grabbed his hand firmly, and with a big smile still on his face (and Phil's, too), walked to the door with me, kissed my cheek, gave me a little hug, and left.

Several minutes later, the doorbell rang. It was Billy. He'd sat in his car thinking and just couldn't drive away. He'd come back, and he wasn't smiling this time. He was fighting tears. He calmly said, "I just had to tell Phil how much he means to me. Is he still up?" I'd moved Phil to the bedroom, so Billy walked in. He grabbed Phil's hand a little tighter this time, he kissed his forehead just a little longer, and he looked into his eyes and said, "Phil, I love you, man. I love you, Phil." Then he left, this time hugging me a little longer. I closed the door.

Five minutes later, the doorbell rang again. This time, when I opened the door, Billy was standing in front of me flooded with tears. He walked right past me and into Phil's bedroom, where Phil was lying down. He fell to his knees and buried his head in Phil's lap and wept. Then he got up, held Phil's hand, and said, "You're my best friend. I love you, and I will see you again." Then Billy walked past me, smiled, and said, "I just had to say good-bye," and he left. That time he went home, and he told everyone he could that they had to hurry and say good-bye to Phil.

Thanks to Billy, in those next two weeks just before Phil passed, many friends came to say their heartfelt good-byes. Phil was so sick, but he mustered up the energy to see all of them, because their love fed his soul, and the love that they shared with each other was so immense. Phil knew when he passed that he would see all of them again.

He knew he was unconditionally loved, and that the greatest of all is love.

Phil's greatest gift to me was always his love. Here is a love letter from Phil, from 2012:

Dear Jennifer, My Sweetheart,

You are a woman of a thousand looks. Wow! Creative in everything you do, photography, video, our beautiful home. You are a mentor to Austin and Jessica. You're sexy and loving. You're caring and appreciative of all of our friends. You're smart and a guiding light for me. Oh, and you're a great dancer. I want to tell you how much I appreciate your love and kindness. Words can't express how special you are in these challenging times. You look fabulous, as always. I'm blessed to say you're my wife. Our spiritual journey has taught us about faith, hope, and love. The greatest of all is love.

I love you.
Phil

Love is invincible. Make love the greatest part of your story.

PHIL-OSOPHY #7

Leave a Legacy

||||||||||||||||||||||||||||||||

A few weeks before Phil passed away, he and I were sitting outside once again watching a hummingbird dance around the feeder in our backyard. He turned to me and whispered, "I have nothing left on my bucket list."

My first thought was just, *Wow*. I said, "Not many fifty-two-year-old men can say that."

He took a deep breath from his oxygen tank. "I've built great companies with a best friend of thirty years. I've been married to the love of my life for twenty-two years. I've guided my beautiful children into adulthood. I have the most amazing friends. I've traveled the world, run marathons, and built homes for homeless families in

Mexico." He paused to take another breath and added, "Just one more thing to do—become the world's greatest grandfather."

Sadly, I knew Phil was not going to achieve his final bucket-list item. But I found great solace in knowing that he had done more in fifty-two years than most people do in their entire lives. He had lived passionately, loved hard, and shared his philosophies with everyone he knew. Every year we would write out the Carroll family mission statement: to live, love, laugh, learn, lead, lend a hand, and leave a legacy of love. In fact, we believe that if you live with purpose and passion, love unconditionally, laugh out loud, learn from your challenges, lead by example, and lend a hand to those in need, you *will* leave a legacy. That is exactly what Phil Carroll did.

The Movie of Phil's Life

Phil died on a Friday, and we had his funeral that Sunday at our local church with our pastors Terry and Judith Crist. Jessica had created a video of Phil's life from our pictures and memories of a rock-star entrepreneur, a loving father, an amazing husband, a devoted friend, a wonderful son, a supportive brother, and an extraordinary man. Throughout this book, I've talked a lot about the story or "the movie" of your life and asked what you wanted to see in it. On this day, I watched an actual movie of Phil's life. As the video began, our beautiful friend Jessica Warren sang "Amazing Grace" with the voice of an angel.

I sat in the front row with Austin on one side and Jessica on the other, surrounded by a church full of people whose lives were touched by this remarkable man. Together we watched the movie of Phil's life on the big screen. We watched footage of him being interviewed back in the Three Buoys days, talking about his vision of seeing the lakes full of houseboats covered in beautiful women in bikinis drinking cocktails.

We saw images of him on stage at his fortieth birthday dressed as Rod Stuart, playing air guitar like a real rocker. Heli-skiing and waterskiing and running marathons and triathlons and traveling the world with his friends. The highlight of the video was the footage of twenty summers spent on the boat with his family, laughing with his kids, teaching them how to wakeboard and waterski and wakesurf and live life out loud.

As the movie of Phil's extraordinary life unfolded, I turned my head, wanting to see how Phil was reacting to this celebration of his life, only to abruptly realize that he wasn't there beside me. This wasn't another birthday party. This was his funeral.

The movie continued with images of Phil dressed up as Santa Claus at Christmas. All the years dressed up in Halloween costumes celebrating Jess's birthday. Shooting pucks with Austin on the ice rink in our backyard in Canada and then on in-line skates on our backyard rink in Arizona.

Once again, getting caught up in this magical movie of his incredible life, I turned to catch a glimpse of Phil's reaction, and once again, I was thrown back into the reality that he was gone from us forever.

Celebrating Phil's Legacy

After the video ended, Jessica, Austin, Ruskin, and I gave our eulogies.

Austin read the Christmas letter Phil received from him days before he died.

Jessica spoke next.

You are the Tomato to my Salad,

You are the Protein to my Shake,
You are the Snow to my Snowboard,
You are the Push to my Pushup,
You are the Wave to my Surf,
You are the Curve to my Smile,
You are the Scuba to my Dive,
You are the Footsteps to my Beach,
You are the Source to my Laughter,
You are the Signature to my Checks,
You are the Lime to my Tequila,
You are the Punchline to my Jokes,
You are the Horizon to my Sky,
And you will always be the first man I ever loved!

There was something about you, Dad, that brought
confidence, energy, and determination into people's
lives! You have touched people's lives you don't even
know. I will miss you forever. I will never stop saying
the word Dad. You will always be on my mind, and you
will always have a special place in my heart. Just as
you taught me, I will never give up. I will always be
your little Scrubber. I promise Mom and Austin and I
will continue to be the mighty, mighty Carrolls.

Then it was Ruskin's turn.

Hello, everyone; for those of you who don't know me,
my name is Ruskin Gallardo. I knew Phil because he
was the second dad in my life. Being around him has

taught me so much in life.

I went through a photo album recently, and there was a photo of Phil lifting me up in the air when I was about one. This was my first time ever seeing this photo, and the first thought that came to mind was, "That is exactly what Phil would do with a one-year-old." And you know what? I am glad he did that with me, because only now do I realize that Phil has been doing that all my life. Eventually I got too heavy for him to literally lift me up, but he still found other ways. My first time trying to waterski, I was too scared to jump in the water because I thought the ogopogo monster would eat me. So Phil decided to jump in with me to give me confidence and help me overcome my fear.

Another time, I was visiting the Carrolls in Arizona, and I met Phil in the kitchen one morning. Phil greets me with a "good morning," and then seconds after, tells me to "catch." As I was trying to remember what the word "catch" meant, I heard an egg crack on the floor in front of me. Phil didn't tell me to clean it up or worry about it; he simply told me to try again, and he threw another one—which I was able to catch. That was just another way Phil lifted me up—whenever I failed, he always told me to try again so that I could succeed.

All my life Phil has been teaching me new things and lifting me up. Enjoying friends, overcoming fears, and not giving up are just a few of the numerous things I learned from Phil. All these moments will be cherished forever. And I know that he probably has his arm around my mom, and they are looking down on Austin, Jessica, and me and saying how proud they are of the people we have become and the great things we will accomplish in the future.

Finally, I got up and walked to the podium.

How could this happen? How could Phil Carroll be taken from us? And how could this be happening again at Christmas? Many of you know that Phil's brother and three cousins were killed Christmas morning twenty years ago. A few weeks ago I was so overwhelmed with the thought that Phil might die at Christmas. So I prayed, and I asked God for his answer.

The next day while hanging ornaments on the Christmas tree with Dolores, I found this box of Christmas bells that Allison gave Phil and me for our wedding, and as I placed one on our tree and heard its ring, something washed over me. God washed over me. I felt the ultimate message from above that we have nothing to worry about. That this life here on earth is a small part of our journey. That Phil is now beginning his endless journey across the other shore where there is peace forever more. He is now reunited with Randi; his cousins, Allison, Greg, and Deanne; his sisters, Dolorn and Maureen; Uncle Dave; Aunt Maureen; Ruskin's mom, Suzanne; and his sister-in-law, Veronica. I imagine him with his arm around his brother, Randi, discussing his ideas on how to restructure heaven. And how to help guide us from above!

Next year when we hear the first Christmas carol, we will not only think about celebrating the birth of our savior Jesus Christ, but also the life of Phil Carroll, a man who made a difference in all of our lives. Phil did a lot of deals in his life, and the last deal he sealed was that we will forever officially be the Christmas Carrolls.

Phil lived his life larger than life. "Go Big or Go Home" was one of his great mottos. He lived life out loud!

If I could summarize Phil's life with a punctuation mark, it would be an exclamation point—eight of them!

But his passing is not the end of Following Phil.

It's not a period.

Think of it as a dot dot dot . . .

A couple weeks before Phil passed away, he shared his bucket list with me—and the only thing left on it was becoming the world's greatest grandpa. We can all only imagine how unbelievable he would have been!

But Phil's grandkids will know him because his brilliance will live on through his children, through me, and through all of you!

We will never stop following Phil. A piece of him is

planted deep into the hearts of every one of us whom he has touched on his journey.

When Phil looked back on his amazing life, what made it remarkable wasn't what he accomplished or where he ventured, but who he spent his life with. So I want to say thank you, from Phil. Thank you for being a valued part of Phil's life. Thank you for loving Phil.

That funeral was a celebration of life. The celebration of a life lived large, a life lived to leave a legacy. But a life not long enough.

The World's Greatest Grandpa

Phil wasn't able to personally cross off his last bucket-list item, but my hope and prayer is that with this book, I can cross it off for him. With this book, Phil's grandchildren can read his stories, learn his Phil-osophies, and talk about him throughout their lives. They'll know their Grandpa Phil and realize he was the world's greatest grandpa, even though they never got to meet him.

But most of all, I wrote this book for my kids, for myself, and for you—to remind us to live our lives *now* to leave a legacy of love.

What will be your legacy? How are you living your life today to leave that legacy?

If your life was cut short, and your significant other was writing your book, or scripting your movie, what philosophies would they share?

How would the movie of your life play out at your funeral? Would it be a celebration of a well-lived life? Who would be in it with you? What would they say about you?

What can you do *right now* to leave your legacy of love and be truly *beyond* invincible?

Get Checked

‖‖‖‖‖‖‖‖‖‖‖‖‖‖‖‖‖‖‖‖‖‖‖‖‖‖‖‖‖

I t was a Thursday night, moments from the end of another long challenging day. I had just finished my nightly cancierge ritual: I had given Phil his various meds, and we had watched some TV together. This was one of my favorite times because Phil would let me cuddle up with him on his reclining bed. His body ached all the time and he hated to be touched, but at night, watching our favorite shows, he let me gently lay my head on his bony shoulder, sometimes with a soft down pillow, but that physical touch was precious to both of us. This man I loved, who used to throw me around a room making wild jungle love, now showed his love and affection with a simple touch that meant so much.

I had brushed his hair with a special brush that didn't irritate his sensitive skin. I had kissed him goodnight on the lips—not once, not twice, but always three long, slow, loving kisses. I had helped lift him up higher on his reclining bed with a "three, two, one, lift," dimmed the lights, and finally said, "Good night, sweetheart." Our master bedroom had been transformed into Phil's hospital room, so I walked down the long hall to Jessica's room. Looking at myself in the mirrored wall, trying desperately to muster up a smile despite my hurting heart.

I felt physically and emotionally exhausted, yet wide awake. I couldn't stop processing the hell of walking through the valley of the shadow of death with Phil. I laid on Jessica's bed in her pretty pink room, staring up at the lime-green ceiling fan, lost in its monotonous spinning. My head was spinning too, filled with so many whys. Why is this happening? Why did he get sick? Why can't we save him? Why is he dying? Why is he leaving us this way? I grabbed my journal and wrote,

December 13, 2012. This sucks! I'm slowly losing my mind. I feel so numb, so surreal, like I am stuck in a dream . . . a nightmare!

Just like every night, I found myself wondering, *Was that the last time I'll brush his hair, the last time he'll whisper my name, our last kiss?* I didn't know on that night, December 13, 2012, the answer to those painful questions was—yes.

Don't Be Afraid

At five o'clock the next morning, my sleep was interrupted by the urgent call of Auntie Gwen: "Jenn, come . . . Phil is dying!" We each took turns monitoring Phil's sleep with a baby monitor.

That night Phil's mom had the monitor and had heard Phil's distressed moaning for help. Running down the hall, we bolted into his room to find Phil slouched over his five-foot-tall mother, who was struggling to hold up his limp body. The doctors had warned us that Phil's cancer had spread dangerously close to his delicate pulmonary artery, and there was a risk that it might burst and end his life. That's probably what happened that morning, although we'll never know for sure.

Phil was in shock. Although he was alert and processing what was going on, he was in distress and struggling to breathe. With his blood pressure falling dramatically, we had to get him back on the bed, which was not an easy task for three ladies. I heard Phil faintly whisper, "Three, two, one." At first, I didn't understand what he meant. Then I remembered our nightly ritual.

I got on the bed behind him, grabbed him tightly yet gently (he moaned from the touch), and instructed Dolores and Gwen to pull him up onto me. Phil nodded in agreement and whispered again so faintly it was more like a groan: "Three, two, one . . . lift." Slowly we inched my six-foot-two husband up onto my chest and onto the bed. We just laid there, exhausted. For the last several months, Phil had been in so much pain that we weren't able to really touch him, but in that strangely mysterious moment, there I was with him lying on top of me, my arms and legs literally wrapped around him, and it didn't seem to cause him pain. Once a 220-pound, strapping hulk of a man, he was a fragile shadow of his former self, dying in my arms. Gwen closely monitored Phil's diminishing heart rate, but everything was eerily peaceful.

We laid there for several minutes before my mom and dad arrived. With one final surge of strength, Phil reached out and grabbed Dad's hand, and Dad spoke those powerful words of comfort, "Don't be afraid!" It was remarkable, but with those words, not only did the heavy weight of fear appear to lift off Phil's shoulders but everyone else's as well. It was as if this wise doctor was giving us all permission to breath and surrender to our ultimate fate. Somehow Dad and Mom's presence just lifted the dark cloud from the room and let the light shine in.

With their help, I was able to slide out from under Phil and get him comfortable in his bed. Then I desperately set out to reach both of my kids and tell them to come home immediately, that their Dad had taken a turn for the worse. As far as they knew, Phil was expected to live until the new year. The very next day, Jessica had plans to fly home to spend Christmas with her dad. Austin was in Calgary playing for the Victoria Royals. He had only two games left, and then he too was heading home.

The end would be very different than what they had anticipated. There would be no more sharing stories, no more presents, and no more laughter. But there also would be no more pain, no more worry, and no more uncertainty. As hard as it is to say good-bye, it's horrible watching someone you love be slowly devoured by disease. You watch them fight with every cell in their body, hoping for an audacious miracle. But in our case, it never came. Phil took one final breath, exhaled it into the air, and his life was over.

Jessica flew in later that day, and when my parents picked her up, they shared the news that shattered her world: her father had died. Later Jessica wrote in her journal:

When we got to our house, all of our closest family and friends were there. I just ran into my mom's arms. It was a scene I had dreaded for a long time.

I decided that I wanted to see my dad. I crawled onto his bed, right next to him. He was always my snuggle

*partner, and I laid my head on his chest and patted his
hair, and noticed for the first time in almost six months
he looked at peace. He wasn't in pain anymore. He
wasn't suffering, and he wasn't trying so hard to just
survive until tomorrow. He looked happy. I could tell
he was in a better place. At that moment I knew that
we don't need to be scared of death, because when we
leave this planet, we're going to be somewhere else—
somewhere miraculous.*

*I laid there for a long time and talked with Dad. I
thanked him for being the most amazing father. I
thanked him for teaching me everything I knew. It was
eerie, but because I knew his time had come and gone,
I was relieved that he took his last breath, because we
just couldn't deal with another day of his suffering.*

To get in touch with Austin, I called my sister Tara, who lives
in Calgary, Canada, where he was playing hockey. She assured me
that she would pick Austin up at the hotel and drive him to the
airport. Later she told me that she did a really strange thing, which
she didn't put much thought into at the time—as she ran out the
door, she grabbed her passport.

It was early in the morning when she reached the hotel to
pick Austin up. Tara drove him to the airport and was getting him
checked in when I texted her that Phil had passed away. I didn't
want her to share that with Austin before his long flight home.

In that moment, my sister decided that she couldn't bear to let
Austin get on the plane without her, so she pulled out her passport
and her credit card and bought a seat on his flight. Phil's sister,
Lisa, who also lived in Calgary, joined Tara and Austin on that

long flight, and together, Austin's two aunts escorted him to see his father for the last time.

It always amazes me how much love comes out during these times. How family and friends end up performing so many little miracles that make such a big difference. I'm so grateful Austin didn't have to be alone on that three-hour flight. Instead, he could laugh and cry with his hilarious aunties.

Austin recalls:

Dad was always on me to write down my expenses for all my hockey road trips. He had been asking me to do this for the last road trip, and I had been procrastinating. So I spent the whole three-hour flight doing a spreadsheet of the expenses of our last trip— which was kind of good, because it got my mind off the fact that my dad was dying. The doctors had kept saying that he was going to be around until the new year, so I really didn't expect to arrive and find out that he had already passed.

At the airport I was met by my mom, our family friends Peter and Melissa Schulof, our driver Ted, and Jessica. The smiles—or rather, fake smiles—on their faces told the story. Dad was gone. We got to the house and it was full of people. I absolutely didn't want to see my dad. I wanted to remember him as the healthy, loving, funny, rock-star man he was. I just didn't want to see my dad dead.

An hour or so passed, and we were all sitting around crying and laughing and sharing stories. It was all

*really weird. Super surreal. My Aunt Lisa, Dad's
sister, took me into the office. She said, "Austin, I lost
my sister. She was badly burned from a car accident.
Everybody saw her and had their time saying good-bye
to her. They were trying to protect me from the horror of
seeing her that way, and I wasn't able to say good-bye.
You know, I regretted it my whole life."*

*She said, "I would rather you go in there and see him
and turn around and come right back out and wish you
hadn't, than let his body be taken away and live like I
have with the regret that you could've spent one last
moment physically together."*

*That was it. Her story changed my mind. I didn't want
to have that regret. I wanted to see his face again, and
the scar on his hand. I wanted to be in his presence. So
I walked in his room and asked everyone to leave. And
I had my moment with my dad. I told him how much I
loved him. It's a moment I don't really want to share. It
is just between us. But I am grateful to have had it.*

WHY?

I often try to make sense of why Phil Carroll—this extraordinary human being who lit up the room, who was all about giving and serving and trying to make the world a better place, who was constantly changing lives, growing businesses, empowering others, and exploring every bit of this extraordinary world we live in— was taken from us at fifty-two. I guess that he had to live large, which also meant dying large. He had to leave a huge legacy, not just with his children and his wife and immediate family, but with so many people. He made the most of everything he had, and he left an imprint on every person whose life he touched. He *had* to live that large.

If that's true, he had to be taken when he was young and vibrant and still had a lot of life left in him—so that not only his life would have significance, but his death would, too. So that Austin, Jessica, and I could continue to share his stories and influence the world in the ways he had. To empower people to not hold back but live large, be positive, and celebrate life. But most significantly, to empower people to live *long*—because in life, length matters! The longer we live in this life, the larger a legacy we can leave. That's what it means to be *beyond* invincible.

Did Dad Do Anything Wrong?

A few days after Phil passed away, the kids and I were driving to pick out Phil's urn when Jessica asked me, "Did Dad do anything wrong?" My first response was, "Oh, of course not, Jess—you know how hard he fought. We had the best doctors. We had the best advice. He did everything he could in his power and wisdom to fight this horrible disease. Of course he didn't do anything wrong."

Then I looked a little deeper into her eyes, and I recognized that this was one of those teachable moments. Those moments when someone asks you something and they don't want the sugar-coated answer. They want the truth. I said to Jessica, "It's not that Dad did anything wrong, but you know Dad—he didn't believe in going to the doctor. Maybe Jessica, just maybe, if Dad had been more proactive about his health, and had yearly physicals like you and I and many others do, maybe he could've been diagnosed early. Maybe that could've saved his life, but we'll never know."

According to the American Cancer Society, one in seven men will be diagnosed with prostate cancer during their lifetime. About one man in thirty-eight will die of prostate cancer. But if detected early, 96 percent of men survive at least fifteen years. Phil Carroll wasn't that guy. He had an invincible spirit, yet he was stopped by what his doctor said was one of the worst cases of prostate cancer he had ever seen.

As you already know, Phil didn't believe in going for regular checkups. He was too busy living large. He ignored obvious symptoms, like urinating more often than other men his age. He thought he was invincible because he ate organic, ran triathlons and marathons, and lived a healthy lifestyle. But he wasn't.

Coach Jeff

Not long before Phil died, I was in Victoria, British Columbia, to watch Austin play for the WHL (Western Hockey League) Victoria Royals and to bring him home to visit his dad for Thanksgiving. While I was in the stands, one of his training coaches, Coach Jeff Compton, came up to me. He spoke solemnly, "I'm sorry—I've heard that your husband is very sick and that he's fighting for his life. May I ask what he has?" I said, "Prostate cancer." He looked at me curiously and said, "Prostate cancer? Gosh, I thought everybody survived prostate cancer. Isn't that the cancer you would choose to get if you had to pick from a list of all the different kinds of cancers?"

I answered, "Yes, as long as you're proactive about your health and you go in and get checked. Surviving prostate cancer depends on early detection. You can be one of the 96 percent of men that survive prostate cancer if it's detected early." Then I looked at Coach Jeff and asked him point blank, "How old are you?" He looked a little rattled and said, "I'm forty-five." I asked, "You do get checked regularly, right?" He kind of sneered and said, "No, no—gosh, I'm in great shape. I'm on the ice with the boys. I don't drink or smoke. Heck, I hate going to the doctor. Certainly I don't need a doctor going *there*," gesturing with his thumb over his shoulder to his buttock region.

Well, it's said that if you're taking care of someone you love while they're dying, you actually go through the phases of grief during the care-giving process. Up until that moment, I hadn't experienced the stage of anger, but uncontrollable anger started bubbling up inside of me. I started to breathe heavily. I started to shake. I looked at this big, burly Canadian hockey coach, and I pointed straight at him.

"What?" I barked, seething. "You go in and you get checked. If you don't do it for yourself, you go get checked for your wife. You go get checked for your kids. So that one day you can walk your daughter down the aisle. You can watch your son play professional hockey. You can grow old with the woman you love. My Phil, he can't do that. He's home and he's sick and he's dying. I don't care if you're afraid or what your excuses are. You go in and you get checked. You bend over and you take it like a man!"

Poor Coach Jeff did not know what hit him. He's used to taking strips off my boy on the ice, but I took a strip off him that day.

Fast-forward three months: Phil had passed away. We had buried him in his hometown of Calgary, Alberta, Canada, beside his three siblings and three cousins. I'm back with Jessica in Victoria, supporting Austin at one of the Royals games.

After the game, Coach Jeff came up to me to express his condolences. Then he kind of looked around and leaned in and whispered to me, "Went in. Got checked. Bent over and took it like a man. You know what, Jenn, as the doctor was putting on his glove, I said, 'Doc, I'm doing this for a woman, and it's not my wife.'"

Gentlemen, I don't want you to have a panic attack over this. I just want you to have a plan of attack, like you do with other aspects of your life. Like your work, or your businesses if you're an entrepreneur. I know the due diligence you put into your deals. You hire a slew of lawyers, pay them way too much, and spend weeks and months examining the deal, and if there's one little red flag, you're out of there. You walk away. Treat your health the way you treat your businesses. Be proactive and get checked.

Ladies, I'm talking to you as well. You too can be proactive about your health. And you can help the men in your life to be, too. We all have an uncle, a brother, a friend, a father, a son, someone we can reach out to with a text, a message, or a phone call. None of the Phil-osophies of life are as important as Get Checked. Reach out to the people you love and tell them, "Be proactive about your health. Get checked. Bend over and take it like a man."

Here is another part of Jessica's journal entry from the day her father died:

Why did God have to take the best man? The man who kept our family alive with his high energy! The first man I ever loved. My best friend. My buddy!

I am scared. What if I forget Dad? What if I forget what his voice sounds like? Or worse, what if I STOP hearing his voice from above? I need his guidance. He is my mentor. Dad always knew what to do. He had all the answers. He gave me confidence. He provided me with tough love.

Love is EVERYTHING! Dad, I am sorry. I know we went on a lot of walks on the beach. I know we went on runs before church (Austin and Mom thought we were cray cray). I know we got to go scuba diving once . . . BUT I WANT MORE! I want to go scuba diving one HUNDRED times with you. I want to go on MORE walks on the beach. I want to go on more runs before church. AND I CAN'T! I don't understand.

You will never meet the love of my life. You will never walk me down the aisle. You will never see the first house I buy. You will never see me host my own show. You will never see my kids. They will never get to call you "Grandpa." Austin and I will miss out on having a dad . . . for the rest of our lives!

Wouldn't You Do Anything for Your Kids?

Dad, will you throw the baseball with me?

Will you watch my dance recital?

Mom, will you fill in my job application with me?

Can you help me learn to drive?

I need some advice about dating.

Dad, will you walk me down the aisle at my wedding?

Dad, will you watch my first NHL hockey game?

Just like you, my Phil would've done anything for his kids. But he can't now because *he's not here.* And my kids feel that pain every day, with every new experience.

Every time I speak in public, every documentary I put together, and every moment I spend writing this book, I imagine my Phil hearing or reading my words, and my only goal is to get through his thick skull—so that one day, another "Phil" might be moved enough to take action, or to share this message so someone else can take action. So that you or your person or your friend might become more proactive about getting checked. So that one life might be saved. So that one young woman won't have to walk down the aisle without her daddy, like my Jessica will have to. So that one young man could hear the shouting of his biggest fan in the crowd as he plays his first professional hockey game. So that one wife of twenty-two years can grow old with the man she loves.

I know you would do anything for your kids. As important as Phil's legacy of living large is, I don't want you to miss the legacy of his death. Be proactive about your health and get checked. Let the movie of your life be long. Be *beyond* invincible.

Finding Our Way

||||||||||||||||||||||||||||||||

*Sometimes the questions are complicated
and the answers are simple.*
–Dr. Seuss

A while back, when Phil was much healthier, the two of us were at Heathrow Airport in London. I couldn't help but notice this man standing confused in the midst of all the craziness—holding up his ticket, looking up at the signs, and then back down at his boarding pass. I was instantly drawn to him; he looked very familiar. Suddenly our eyes locked, and he walked right up to me, stretched his hands out to grasp mine, and said humbly, "Hello, I'm Deepak Chopra."

Standing before us was one of the world's greatest spiritual leaders, right there in the flesh.

Holding his hand, star struck, I responded, "So thrilled to meet you, Mr. Chopra! We've read so many of your books, we do your meditations, and we've even seen you speak, twice. You look much larger on stage, I must say." I gasped as I clasped my hands over my mouth, shocked that my inner voice had allowed me to blurt out those words.

I quickly stammered, "You've enlightened our lives; thank you so much!"

"You are so very, very welcome," Deepak responded politely, then anxiously added, "but could you help me? I seem to be lost."

"Of course," I answered. "Let me see your boarding pass."

I took a quick look. "Mr. Chopra, you're in the wrong terminal. You're in terminal C. You need to go to terminal F. It's simple: just go down the hall, take a left, and get on the connection train. It'll take you to your terminal."

"Thank you very, very much," he said, as Phil and I watched him walk away down the busy corridor towards the train and disappear in the crowd.

I looked at Phil and said, "Do you understand what just happened? We just showed one of the most enlightened men alive . . . his way!"

In that moment, I realized we could all lose our way, even Deepak Chopra. Where do we go? What do we do? How do we live our lives to leave our legacy? Those are complicated questions, but maybe the answers are simpler than we think.

Alone and Afraid

It's been five years since I lost my way—since I lost my Phil. I found myself alone and afraid in a world I'd not made. The first year, I was basically numb. Just recovering and recuperating from the horrific experiences of walking beside the one I loved as he fought for his life and watching him die.

Since then, I've walked alone on many beaches, watched a lot of hummingbirds, and done a lot of reminiscing about Phil and our beautiful life together. I've discovered how much of my life revolved around Phil, and how our family and I have been forced into a new way of being—alone. At forty-nine, I had no choice but to pull up my big-girl panties (okay, my Victoria's Secret pink lace thongs) and set off down a new road and discover Jenn again. A new Jennifer. A Jenn without Phil.

I've rekindled a relationship with myself, but it hasn't been easy. I've journaled a lot over the last several years and even wrote some poetry to express my deep inner feelings and realizations. There's been anxiety and fear and panic attacks and waking up in cold sweats, wanting so badly for all of this to just be a nightmare. Hoping I could roll over and cuddle with Phil again and have him reassure me that it's all going to be OK.

Taking the "ID" out of W*id*ow

Since Phil's passing, I spent four and a half years dealing with his probate. Despite being a financial genius, Phil did not, as they say, "have his things in order." This was proof positive that Phil did not believe he was going to die. I could write a book on how to prepare yourself in the unlikely event of your spouse's sudden death. *He Got Hit by a Bus: Now What?* might be a great title.

After twenty-four years of being in a relationship, I am now single and trying to date—keyword "trying." I've learned tips for Tinder. Amidst all the challenges of dating at fifty, I've learned how to take the "ID" out of *widow* and discover my *wow*. Although I'm open to finding love again, and I know Phil would want that for me, I do think of him constantly. His Phil-osophies of life guide Austin, Jessica, and me every day.

I have discovered Jenn again by staying positive, celebrating life, and more than ever, realizing that love is all that matters. The love of my children and my parents and Phil's parents and all of my incredible friends is what has pulled me through this darkness and allowed me to find the light—find my light.

Six months after Phil passed away, Jenny Locklin, president of Chats Toastmasters Club, asked if I would represent our club in an international speaking contest with my "Chuck-It Bucket" speech.

It was exactly what I needed. I was able to muster up all of my confidence and energy, share our story just months after Phil passed away, and win the competition for Chats. With that, I sprung back to life.

Shortly afterwards, I was approached by the Entrepreneur Organization to write an article for *Octane* magazine about Phil and his life. The article was titled "Go Big or Go Home." As a result of that magazine article, I got a call from our good friend Mathew Stewart, an EO member in Orange County, who was chairing the Argentinean EO University and wanted me to speak and share Phil's story. Initially, I was supposed to be presenting to just the spouses in a breakout session. The message soon spread around the convention that I was sharing our story, and they had to move me to a different room to accommodate the hundred-plus people who crammed in to hear Phil's story. I received a standing ovation and ended up with the highest speaker ranking of anyone at the university.

Then I was invited on a three-week tour through India to speak at different EO chapters. My good friends and EO members, Aanchal and Karan Bhatia, hosted Jessica and me for one of the most incredible trips of our lives. The highlight was undoubtedly having an audience with none other than the Dalai Lama at his ashram in Dharamsala. Jessica, Aanchal, and I, along with three other women we had met along our Indian journey, spent a treasured thirty minutes talking, laughing, and crying with His Holiness.

When Jessica asked him how she, a twenty-two-year-old girl, could make a difference, he looked her deeply in the eyes and responded, "You must preach that we are all ONE, without boundaries or judgment." Those profound words have come to be the mantra of our lives.

I am grateful for the tremendous support the Entrepreneur Organization has given me and my family. It was only after seeing the incredible effect Phil's story has had on so many people at EO speaking events that I found the passion to share his Phil-osophies of life in the form of this book, to share them with the world.

What Do You Want?

One day recently, when Austin was in the bathroom brushing his teeth, I went in to chat with him about our day together. I saw that he had written in big, bold letters with a red marker across his mirror, "What do you want?"

I was in awe. It was such a Phil thing to do. I looked at him and said, "What *do* you want, Austin?" He answered, point blank, "I want to make the NHL." Then he paused and whispered two words that sent chills down my spine. "Like breath."

"What do you mean?" I asked.

"Like I need my next breath, Mom; that's how much I want to make the NHL."

I was speechless and so empowered by his conviction.

Then he looked at me and asked, "Mom, what do *you* want?" Imagining what I might want as much as my next breath, I answered, "Austin, I want to share Dad's story. I want to share our story with the world and save lives. I want to bring meaning not only to Dad's life but to his death."

A good friend of Phil's and mine, Mark Moses, whom we've known through EO for twenty-five years, has a company called CEO Coaching International. As a valued part of our team, he's helping to coach Jessica and me on our "Live Long" mission to save lives. One of the exercises he had us do was to imagine looking into a crystal ball and write out what we envisioned, as a way to answer that very complicated question, "What do you want?"

It turned out to be an easy exercise for me. When I looked into my crystal ball, I saw a man putting on a bow tie. He's getting dressed in a tuxedo because he's going to a wedding. He picks up the phone and calls me and says, "Hi, Jennifer. You don't know me, but I've read your book, and I was inspired by your message. I went in, I got checked, and I found out I had prostate cancer. I've been treated and I'm a survivor. I'm about to go walk my daughter down the aisle at her wedding and do a daddy-daughter dance. I wanted to call you and thank you for making a difference in my life."

If I could make only one copy of this book and give it to just one person, it would be to my Phil ten years ago. Phil lived his life every day to leave a legacy. He continues to leave his legacy. He continues to be invincible. Right now, my legacy is to be Phil's significant "significant other" by sharing his Phil-osophies of life with you to inspire you to take action. To live large by celebrating life, being positive, leaving no words unspoken, and living to give. And to live long by getting checked, being proactive about your health, and bending over and taking it like a man.

Hummingbird Magic

It was just another morning in Scottsdale, sunny and hot. I opened the door to our backyard, and Dill, my little Shih Tzu doggy, rushed out and immediately started playing with something on the ground by the window. It was a hummingbird. A beautiful, turquoise-feathered hummingbird, sprawled out on its back, lying lifeless. I gathered the little thing up in my hand and just held it. Deep waves of profound sadness washed over me. I stood there caressing the bird's wings and weeping uncontrollably.

As I have shared with you, during Phil's cancer journey, that little magical dancer I held limp in my hand had come to represent hope, love, and time standing still. It brought with it appreciation for living in the now, savoring peaceful moments watching and listening to the whispers of God. During my dark days of grief following Phil's death, the tiny birds seemed to buzz into my space at the precise moments I needed to see their flicker of light.

I cried out loud, "Why did it have to die?"

I could hardly see through my pools of tears. I kept petting the precious bird as if I were stroking Phil's hair. "I'm so sorry, little one. I'm so sorry that you had to die." And in that moment of immense grief, I confessed all the thoughts I had wanted to share with Phil since his passing. "I don't know what to do! I feel so lost and afraid without you. Why did you die? Why did you leave us? I'm so sorry!"

It was as if I was holding Phil in my arms again as he fought for his last breath. It was at that moment, holding that tiny little bird in my hands, that I hit rock bottom. I felt so broken, hopeless, alone, afraid, and full of complicated questions.

Suddenly, in an instant, it all changed. Something miraculous happened. That little hummingbird opened its eyes. It was not dead; it was merely dazed and confused. For a moment it just stared at me, deeply into my soul like Phil did at the end. In sheer disbelief, I frantically started wiping away the tears so I could see more clearly. It levitated and hovered above my hand for mere seconds, almost in a moment of gratitude. Then it flew off.

I was dumbfounded! It hadn't died in my arms like Phil did. It lived and it flew away and it started a new life—a new beginning.

I watched as it soared high into the sky above, and as the sun shone down on my face, I felt the message from Phil and God: *I must open my eyes. I must spread my wings and fly away on my new journey of life.* Yes, I lost Phil, and it was horrible and it was devastating and it was wrong and it was sad. Yet I did not lose my life—my self. Just like that beautiful turquoise hummingbird, I too needed to fly away.

I grabbed my two little Shih Tzu doggies, loaded up my truck, and drove to Beverly . . . Hills, that is: swimming pools and movie stars and my daughter Jessica. The next week, I put my house up for sale. The house Phil and I raised our children in for fifteen years. Those days were behind me now, and I needed to start a new story. I had to fly away like my hummingbird with hope and love and time standing still.

That's where I am today. This book is my story. It is my truth. It is the story of a rock-star entrepreneur, an epic love affair, and the lessons we learned living while dying. Like breath, I want this message to save lives.

No one is insulated from challenge, chaos, or even catastrophe. I wasn't, and neither are you. Even Deepak Chopra loses his way!

Life is constantly bombarding us with complicated questions: Where do we go? What do we want? How do we live our lives to leave our legacy of love? How do we become invincible?

Maybe, just maybe, the answers are simply the Phil-osophies of life: to be positive, celebrate life, leave no words unspoken, just keep swimming, live to give, get checked. And, of course, love is all that matters.

Maybe these simple answers are the only ones you need to leave *your* legacy and truly be invincible.

GRATITUDE ROCKS

Phil used to collect rocks from beaches around the world. He called them gratitude rocks. He wanted us to put them in pockets and purses and in the top drawer of desks, so that every time we stumbled across them, we would pause and reflect on how grateful we were for the many blessings of life.

As I sit here holding a gratitude rock in my hand, I feel tremendously grateful to so many people who have made such a significant impact on our lives.

More than ever, I have come to appreciate that it's not what we do in life, but who we do it with that makes all the difference. So many people have loved and supported Phil, me, and our family on this journey of life, loss, and bouncing back.

To Jessica: Thank you for being a dream daughter (and my roommate for the past year!) and loving and supporting me every step of this storytelling journey. The countless hours you spent listening to me read, cry, rewrite, and read again motivated me to keep going. I look forward to continuing our journey of speaking together around the world, sharing our Beyond Invincible message . . . the J&J Way!

To Austin, my dream son: Thanks for standing so tall and strong through these challenging years without Dad. You are unequivocally the rock of this family. You told me, after reading my manuscript for the third time, "Mom, I know you want this book to change the world and save lives, but even if it doesn't go as big as you imagine, just know that to the world this might only be one book, but to me this book means the world." Because of your words, whatever happens, this book is already a huge success! Thank you for the gift of gratitude.

To my parents, Joanne and Peter Whidden: Thank you for a lifetime of unconditional love and unwavering support. Thanks for being with me every step of my journey through life, both the good times and the bad. I'm so grateful that you read and reread my numerous drafts of this book. I truly won the parent lottery.

To my sister, Tara Mathison: Thank you for always taking care of me like a big sister would, even though you are the younger one. You are so wise and have brought so much joy and laughter to my life, especially since Phil passed. I love you so much.

To my brother, Paul Whidden: Sadly, we both have had to experience losing a spouse. Thank you for being such a great support and role model to me, showing me that there is life and love after loss. You and Michelle give me tremendous confidence that I too will find love again and that life does goes on.

To my in-laws, Dolores and Lorne Carroll, and Phil's sister, Lisa: Thank you for continually showing me the importance of faith. Your remarkable strength through life's ups and downs is inspirational. The Phil-osophies of life I write about in this book were inherited from you. You are truly remarkable.

To Gwen Pogue: You are such a blessing to this world and everyone who loves you. Thank you for being Phil's nurse and for adding such a devout spiritual presence to our lives. God works his magic through you in everything you do.

To Phil's team of outstanding doctors and surgeons: Thank you for your unwavering patience and commitment to helping Phil fight for his life. Thanks especially to Dr. Andrew Buresh, oncologist, Arizona Center for Cancer Care; Dr. Paul Andrews, urologist, Mayo Clinic Phoenix; Dr. Irene Taw, radiation oncologist; Dr. Richard Sue, critical care specialist, St Joseph's Hospital; Dr. Michael Roberts, oncologist; and Dr. Ethan Bindelglas. A special shout-out to Dr. Peter G. Whidden, father-in-law, and Dr. Elbert Kuo, thoracic surgeon, for evaluating, interpreting, and guiding Phil's medical treatment options—you were his most valued players on the team! You thought he was Superman, and that made all the difference.

To Dave Steele, Phil's other life partner (second wife, no benefits—LOL): You were a brother to Phil, but also my big hairy angel during the toughest years. Thank you for always bringing humor and laughter into even the darkest of days. Never stop cracking yourself up, because we'll always laugh along with you.

To our people: Misty and Scott Vogtritter, Lynn and Neil Balter, Sherry Steele, Debra and Tony Nissley, Bridgette and Howie Long, Billy Trimble, Lisa Cohen, Gary Castrucci, Janet and Sean Lambert, Melissa and Peter Schulhof, Janet and Danny Nasser, Rita and Peter Thomas, Sharron and Larry Rosenberg, Ron Mathison, Lori Mottlowitz, Vince Poscente, Sunita Singh, Pat Delesalle, Steve Jillings, Cathy Trimble, Max Cohen, Ted Lang, Brent Barker, and Veronica Valencia (RIP). Thank you for being a constant stream of love, support, and laughter in our lives. Phil was always proud of his "dysfunctional friends." He truly felt like a rock star when he was celebrating life with you all over the world!

To my speaking mentor Joel Weldon and my Chats Toastmasters family: thank you for empowering me to discover my voice and teaching me the art of impactful storytelling. Those fifteen years of tough-love coaching made a difference.

To the Entrepreneur Organization: thank you for showing Phil and me the world and continuing to be a valued part of my life of learning.

To everyone else mentioned in this book: you are and always will be a valued part of our lives. Thank you for making a difference to such a great man. Like Phil, your love is beyond invincible.

Thanks to my remarkable editor, Amanda Rooker, for brilliantly helping me bring our story to life in the pages of this book.

Thanks to David Hancock, Jim Howard, and the Morgan James Publishing team for your commitment to excellence.

Most of all, thank you, Phil, for all the gratitude rocks, for continuing to be the wind beneath our wings, and for being *beyond* invincible.

ABOUT THE AUTHOR

Jennifer L. Carroll is an in-demand motivational speaker, author, and documentarian whose passion is to inspire others to laugh, live large, live long, and leave a profound legacy. She received her bachelor's degree in broadcast journalism from Arizona State University, has been a TV news reporter and entertainment host for Global Television Network and CTV  Television Network, and is the author of the children's book *Bigsbee's Unbee-lievable Journey to Fly.* An avid snowboarder, wake surfer, cyclist, and yogi, Jennifer loves to dance, travel, and entertain her lifelong friends with her storytelling. Mother to YouTube influencer/on-camera host Jessica Carroll and professional hockey player Austin Carroll, Jennifer lives in Scottsdale, AZ, with her two dogs Gigi and Dill.

To connect with Jennifer, and for a deeper look into the life and times of the Carrolls, visit www.JenniferLCarroll.com.

Morgan James
Speakers Group

www.TheMorganJamesSpeakersGroup.com

We connect Morgan James published
authors with live and online events
and audiences who will benefit
from their expertise.

Morgan James makes all of our titles available
through the Library for All Charity Organization.

www.LibraryForAll.org